Acknowledgments

Introduction

| | | |
|---|---|---|
| 1 | Wizard of Oz | 1 |
| 2 | Friend of Bill W. | 12 |
| 3 | Keep Coming Back | 27 |
| 4 | Hope for Cherokee | 41 |
| 5 | Empty Smile | 54 |
| 6 | Face Down Phone | 68 |
| 7 | D-Day February 12, 2020 | 78 |
| 8 | Modern Day Leprosy | 90 |
| 9 | Shame on You | 103 |
| 10 | Morning after Pill | 115 |
| 11 | The Devil Amongst Us | 126 |
| 12 | Fight | 138 |
| 13 | Prodigal | 150 |

# ACKNOWLEDGMENTS

Mike S, Tim R, Rick Ruppe, and Harril W Who, because of their love and reaching out when I needed it most without them, I would have surely crumbled under shame. Because of their love, My faith is alive, and this book was possible

Erica, Luke, Joy, Krissy C, Matt, and Tammy checked in on me, listened to me, and showed me love when I was at my lowest.

Jeff, Karen, Nick, Sean, with their love, I am still clean and sober; they exhibited the finest attributes of our beloved program.

Kirby homegroup, especially Sam giving me a Christian home.

My parents, without their support and love, I would have been lost.

Alisha P helped me crawl out of my shame, showed me the Good in me when all I saw was bad in myself, and showed me this book could be possible.

Blas C, Chad G, Shawn P, Joey M and all my brothers in the Samson society

Elizabeth and Ninette, and everyone I worked with at Walgreens, being there was one of the best experiences of my life.
My son Ben loved me and was my only reason for existence for many months; I lived solely to pick you up and spend time with you. I love you.

My ex-wife had borne the burden of my sin more than anyone else and yet continued to treat me with respect and put our children first.
Erin, I love you and will always be here and want to be your Dad again. I love you and miss you

My Lord and Savior Jesus Christ, who was with me in the darkest confines of my soul as I swallowed the darkest parts of shame, I am beautiful, and I am a child of God.

"The Thorn"
by Martha Snell Nicholson

I stood a mendicant of God
before His royal throne
And begged him for one priceless gift,
which I could call my own.
I took the gift from out His hand,
but as I would depart
I cried, "But Lord, this is a thorn
and it has pierced my heart.
This is a strange, a hurtful gift,
which Thou hast given me."
He said, "My child, I give good gifts
and gave My best to thee."
I took it home and though at first
the cruel thorn hurt sore,
As long years passed, I learned at last
to love it more and more.
I learned He never gives a thorn
without this added grace,
He takes the thorn to pin aside
the veil which hides His face.

# INTRODUCTION

The church is broken in many ways. Years of pleasantries and hollow worship dependent on tradition while keeping appearances up have proven ineffective for those who struggle with sin. While in church, one would almost get the impression that well-mannered church folk are immune from the secular world's temptations and struggles. The struggles of the world are the same struggles of the church; sin is nothing new. I struggled with my faith for many years, once brought to my knees by my alcoholism. I found a relationship with God in the rooms of recovery and began attending church, heavy with the burden of pornography addiction. The physical affair that followed and its revelation in the cruelest of manners would test my faith and my view of the church and force me to my knees again. I became desperate for the love of Christ.

I was married to a wonderful woman for almost twenty years who honored her vows and loved me more than I deserved; she stood by me through multiple deployments while serving in the Marine Corps. She tried to help me and stood by my side with my alcoholism when nobody else did. She picked up the slack when I went to recovery meetings in my early sobriety and whisked the kids away so I could complete my schoolwork while in college and graduate school. She withstood my childish outbursts when I was learning to mature in my thirties. Despite her love and loyalty all those years, I had an affair with a bitter woman high on drugs for a couple of years. This book is my attempt for reparation and to make use of the suffering I have caused.

I will be introducing my struggles with my faith and my addictions to you, but I will not get into any vulgar details. I have heard it said we write to find a solution to a problem; that is what I am doing to find a solution. If this book can open the conversation between the church and people who struggle the way I have, I strongly suspect I am not alone—it will all be worth it. Please open your heart and keep an open mind; this is my story.

Not everything in this book paints the modern church positively, but I can assure you it is written with the utmost sincerity and love. My intentions are pure and without malice in my heart. This book is my way of rectifying all the self-absorbed destruction I have caused all the people I love. I have made many decisions based solely on myself, counter to the teachings of our Savior.

I feel the church is dying from within. Part of the reason is our hypersexualized society, killing the men we love in the church. I am nobody special; I hold no pastoral degrees or prestigious appointments. I am just a struggling Christian trying to voice my love for Christ and help even one person preserve their family. My addictions and my selfish actions have brought nothing but pain to those I love. Let's uncover what I believe is the unspoken cancer in our church eating the men from within. We have many new words or labels, which I will use throughout this book. I feel sometimes they are just synonyms for what my issue is: sin. I have a sin problem, plain and simple, and if I use words like "addict," "alcoholic," "narcissist," or any other label, I do not intend to detract from that; it is a sin, pure and straightforward. Ecclesiastes 1:9 says, "What has been will be again, what has been done will be done again; there is nothing new under the sun" (NIV).

These are not new problems. They are as old as time, and I believe, as Fyodor Dostoevsky said, "There is only one thing that I dread: not to be worthy of my sufferings." I know Jesus loves me, but maybe I can love others through sharing this story.

# 1 WIZARD OF OZ

I grew up in Rhode Island, and the only faith I had ever known was Catholicism. There were no other denominations that I was aware of; you were Catholic or didn't go to church. I remember the Catholic Church in West Warwick, Rhode Island. It was a beautiful church, and I was always impressed by it. It was ornate, and there was plenty of visual stimulation for young eyes in that church. Statues, plaques, some even in Latin: the church had a plethora of eye candy. The church had wood strewn throughout and was incredibly ornate. The most prominent feature was the wooden cross of the crucified Christ above the altar. I remember how beautifully carved it was. The detail was impressive.

The carved statue of the crucified Christ above the altar frightened me. It was symbolic of my faith for many years. The eyes were piercing; no matter where you were in the Church, Jesus seemed to look right at you. Even more than at you, it was like a soul-penetrating stare. He knew me and everything I was doing. I thought if I never looked at Him, He seemed to leave me alone. For about forty-five minutes, I would not make eye contact with the statue. Instead, I looked at less threatening trinkets throughout the church. Yet, I looked like I was paying attention when the Priest gave his sermon. As long as I did, I was fine and had done my Christian duty for the week.

I remember my mom singing gospel hymns while ironing. She was always remarkably more vibrant after mass and oddly annoying. Like throwing pancakes at a wall, some memories stick more than others. I know Christ put me on this path for a reason—like Paul had to be Saul first to be Paul. He had to endure his past for a better future.

I am not a big religious thinker. Still, I know I had to endure many years of distance from God, and looking back, I realize He threw me many life preservers along the way, but I stayed on the monkey bars long after my arms were tired. Throughout the Bible, God picks the troubled and the lonely. There is no way to enjoy the light unless you have been completely immersed in the dark.

We would come home to my ex-wife's hometown and go to the church of her youth—the same one where we got married. I would mainly sit in the church staring at the trinkets and such, not paying much attention. It was a small church, and they ran through preachers like no tomorrow. This Sunday, they had a new young preacher. I always enjoyed fishing, and this particular Sunday, he was preaching on John 21:6.

*"He said, 'Throw your net on the right side of the boat, and you will find some.' When they did, they were unable to haul the net in because of the large number of fish" (NIV).*

He kept preaching on the fact that Jesus draws us, pulls us into His service. I cannot remember the entire message, but I was utterly fixated on his every word instead of half-sleeping. It was just like when Dorothy landed in Oz, and everything went to color. It was a feeling that came over me that I cannot fully explain, but I know God was drawing me.

I was suddenly a believer; I believed in Jesus! I remember leaving the church that day feeling refreshed. Nothing else had changed about me. I was still a drunk. I was still a liar. I was still manipulative. I was still a sinner, but I believed in Jesus. Even the Apostle Paul, who wrote two-thirds of the entire New Testament, said in Romans

7:15-20,

*"I do not understand what I do. For what I want to do, I do not do, but what I hate I do. And if I do what I do not want to do, I agree that the law is good. As it is, it is no longer I myself who do it, but it is sin living in me. For I know that good itself does not dwell in me, that is, in my sinful nature. For I have the desire to do what is good, but I cannot carry it out. For I do not do the good, I want to do, but the evil I do not want to do—this I keep on doing. Now, if I do what I do not want to do, it is no longer I who do it, but it is sin living in me that does it"* (NIV).

If the Apostle Paul struggled, there is hope for someone like me. I believed but was still spiritually and emotionally immature. It takes time to grow, and sometimes—at least with my story—I only learn with pain. I believed and started to act like I thought Christians should behave. I cut out lousy language, started reading the Bible, and memorized Scripture. I began rebuking those, especially my ex-wife, who didn't live up to my Christian ideals. I was a paper deacon, full of faith but still reeking of alcohol. It was ego-driven; I was trying to impress others.

It is one thing to admit you are a sinner saved by grace, but it is entirely a different ballgame to put that admission into action. I believed Jesus was going to come down and magically straighten out my life. Although I was a believer, I began to lose faith. I continued drinking my self-created magic Kool-Aid mixed with vodka. I started to fool people into thinking I had become a good Christian man--except my ex-wife, who saw through my Christian mirage the entire time. Even after Dorothy's world turned to color, she still had to follow the yellow brick road and go through the haunted forest.

Through all my Christian walks, I have been battling addictions in some form or another. Just as the wicked witch was chasing Dorothy, my addictions to alcohol, porn, and sexual immorality hunted me. Jesus would surely come to remove my temptations, or so I thought.

1 Corinthians 10:13 says, *"No temptation has overtaken you except what is common to mankind. And God is faithful; he will not let you be tempted beyond what you can bear. But when you are tempted, he will also provide a way out so that you can endure it"* (NIV).

Maybe our battles define us. I used to hear countless times in meetings and from my sponsor, "pain is growth." It became almost cliché to listen to it. I used to ponder its significance to my current struggle because of the simple recurrence of such phrases as that. But it is true. Pain lets us feel the byproduct of our transgressions, but we are often growing in our faith because we deny ourselves what we know isn't good for our relationship. I will not be tempted or put into any pain beyond what others before me have felt.

When you come from the spiritual basement such as I was and suffer from severe spiritual immaturity as I did, it is hard not to look beyond what is in front of you. That moment in that church, when suddenly I believed, wasn't but the first small step in a long line of small divine experiences. The key to open that door is a willingness to look outside yourself for a solution. The entrance to our heart does not have to be open much for the love of God to penetrate its cold exterior. I was not much of a changed man after that moment, and looking back, my conversion was and is still ongoing.

I don't doubt the power of the Holy Spirit, but I know myself. I question when one claims instantaneous and miraculous transformation. I have heard people tell me that Jesus healed them many times, and they are the most boisterous in church. My faith, in many ways, is like a muscle. It was weak and unformed initially, and just like an immature young boy, I would flex my pathetic muscle of faith and pretend it was much bigger than it was, but I was fooling myself. For the first time in my life, I began reading the Bible cover to cover. The Bible in my home was always on the bookshelf but rarely opened. You would receive a Catholic Bible when you got married and would only open it when a close relative died, and you placed a Catholic pamphlet from the funeral in the Bible.

As I began to read the Bible, I became excited because many of those stories were new to me. I knew the main characters of the Bible, but to read it in its entirety was exhilarating, and I started to feel connected to God. At thirty-two years old, I had a child-like faith, but I was still drinking and living a cleaned-up alcoholic's life. I was a barstool preacher. Nothing sicker in this world than someone who believes they are not emotionally sick but healed, and they reek of vodka. In retrospect, I can only imagine the mental anguish this may have caused my ex-wife to hear the one she is paired with speak of high morality but still live the life of an alcoholic.

Sitting in the church amongst the good Christian families, I was comforted into believing the outside presentation of those around me and so desperately wanted to fit in. Brennan Manning said in *The Ragamuffin Gospel*: "The temptation of the age is to look good without being good." I wanted to be saved and found right then and didn't want to have hard conversations with myself and humble myself to the point of asking for help. But I also didn't want to deny myself anything I wanted because that would take discipline, of which I had little. [1]

---

[1] Brennan Manning, The Ragamuffin Gospel (Colorado Springs, CO: Multnomah Books, 2015).

My family and I regularly attended a local Methodist church and eventually joined a couple's class. I was instantly impressed with the men in the class. I became enthralled and watched them with great amazement—how they carried themselves, how they treated their wives and their humble confidence. I put on an excellent Christian show around them. I thought to myself that if I acted like them, I could be like them. I had good intentions but wanted a more comfortable, softer way. It takes a lifetime to mature as they did, and I didn't see but a small snippet of their life every week.

Humility is being who you genuinely are around others and especially in front of God. I was a fake, a liar, and a drunk. I wasn't courageous enough to show people who I was. I needed help in every way you could think of, but I was too busy orchestrating my illusion in hopes Jesus was going to send a miracle. It would come many times, but not in the way I wanted it. Despite my best efforts or non-efforts, I knew a storm was brewing, and I slowly began to distance myself from my ex-wife and young daughter. In those days, I tried to keep everyone in my life on borderline insanity.

There was a clean-up day happening at the church. A Sunday School teacher I was particularly impressed with signed up to volunteer. So I changed my name on the roster to ensure I was on the same team as him. I had gone to recovery meetings several months before and had arrogantly deemed them "not Christ-like enough." I was still attending the meetings but armed with my Bible and self-conceit. I considered my vast knowledge of reading the Bible from cover to -cover far superior to those poor saps at the recovery meetings who knew nothing about true religion.

I truly believed I was exceptional, and if you didn't believe me, you could ask me. I would gladly tell you. Yet, some members had been sober for up to thirty years. They were utterly devoted to helping others with their recovery. Many had become pillars of their community and families.

Despite my arrogance, I knew my life was in shambles, and I was too prideful and stupid to see the answer that was in front of me. Jesus would not come down on a magic carpet and whisk away my problems, but I was still hurting. I decided to ask my Sunday School teacher what I should do to fix my life correctly. After watching him closely for several months, I wanted everything he had. I was confident he had the answers I was looking for; even though the meetings have helped over six million people recover from addiction, I was convinced this man had the answers I needed. As the clean-up day drew closer, I practiced in my head over and over what I was going to tell him. I would let him know what I was struggling with as a brother of Christ; with his vast knowledge of the Bible, he had to know the answer and what I needed to do to stop drinking.

When the day came, I followed him around like a puppy, always by his side. I was working up the courage to unload on him my difficulties for his analysis. Life just seemed to bless him and his family, and I wanted what he had. Later in the day, we were raking the church's backyard; it was just the two of us. Here was my chance. I stopped raking. I told him everything. For the first time in my life, I was candid with another man about where I was in my life with no reservations. I told him about the drinking, the hiding, the lying, the manipulation, and so much more. He stopped raking and listened intently. Judging from his facial expressions and body language, I had his full attention.

I finished and waited for what I thought was to come, our eyes locked. Instead, he grasped the rake again and continued raking, and a moment later looked at me and said, "Why don't you just stop buying the alcohol if it's such a problem in your life? "I had made him uncomfortable, and we continued to rake in silence. We finished up what we had to do, and he gave me a fatherly pat on the back before I left the church. I was utterly devastated at that moment, and it quickly snuffed out my burning faith to a lukewarm ember. I felt rejected. Alcohol had become my savior and Lord at this stage. Simply suggesting that I minimize an errand, make a budget cut completely ignored how mentally and physically dependent on it, I indeed was.

My reaction to feelings of dejection and abandonment by this man and the entire church—and Christ himself is the byproduct of my spiritual immaturity.

C.S. Lewis writes in Mere Christianity, *"...result I have a reluctance to say much about temptations to which I myself am not exposed. No man, I suppose, is tempted to every sin. It so happens that the impulse which makes men gamble has been left out of my make-up, and no doubt, I pay for this by lacking some good impulse of which it is the excess or perversion. I, therefore, did not feel myself qualified to give advice about permissible and impermissible gambling: if there is any permissible, for I do not claim to know even that."* [2]

Looking back with just a smidgen more spiritual development, I can see that the man I'd approached knew nothing of addiction and knew nothing of my problems. I had falsely put that man on a throne. Like Dorothy's friends in the Wizard of Oz, the wizard we seek may not be the correct one, and what we seek may already be within our grasp. With honest reflection, it's apparent

---

[2] C. S. Lewis, *Mere Christianity* (Harpercollins Publishers, 2017).

Jesus, and especially the church had not abandoned me. They had been guiding me to the path they believed I should follow.

Before honest reflection, however, I seriously began to doubt the church. Maybe it wasn't for me. I once, years before, used to sneak to the old wood road and drink. Through the woods, I could see a church; I used to go early Sunday morning and pretend I was fishing. I would see all the friendly, nicely dressed church people and their perfect families going to worship. I believed that good church people were born with that "good person" gene for a long time, and I wasn't. Those feelings of inferiority came sweeping back to me with a vengeance. I tried my go at being a good Christian, and apparently, I failed. Jesus must not love me as I couldn't stop drinking. My life was spiraling out of control, and obviously, I was not good enough to get sober in a twelve-step recovery program, seemingly not worthy of being a good Christian.

I sat and drank at my insecure pity party for an extended amount of time. I never needed many excuses to feel sorry for myself and whine a bit about how the world had wronged poor Ricky. In retrospect, that man I dumped my guts to tried to talk to me and even told me he was praying for me. It was me who had been cold. I don't know how my ex-wife tolerated the social immaturity I displayed in public. —My thought is she would blame it on me being a Yankee. It was, and is, that I was immature and self-absorbed.

Matthew 23:9-10 says, *"And do not call anyone on earth 'father,' for you have one Father, and he is in heaven. Nor are you to be called instructors, for you have one Instructor, the Messiah" (NIV).*

I continued to pretend to be a good Christian man; I enjoyed the attention it brought. But I was a long way from an honest, sincere religious walk with Christ. I honestly believe I was fooling everyone; I had become the bleeding deacon who reeked of gin. I put myself on a spiritual platform above those around me in the recovery meetings, oblivious that those poor unbelievers were getting better. They were getting sober and staying sober. They were getting their lives together, and mine was getting worse by the day. I continued to ask people in recovery for help but would fail even to try to follow the suggestions to stay sober one day at a time. I once picked up a two-month sober chip while drunk and gave a tearful speech thanking Jesus; they let me finish, thanked me, and told me to keep coming back.

  Have you ever met a man who lights up the room and changes everyone's behavior with few or no words? The work environment's whole dynamic changed because of this one particular man who was firm in his faith, not in his words. His whole aura exuded the love of Jesus. He seemed to bring the best out in people without even putting effort into it. He made being a Christian seem natural and effortless. When he walked into the room, the vulgar and tasteless conversation changed not because of his demands but because people naturally respected him.

  Morning Bible studies began at my work when he arrived; I began attending, and looking back, I learned more about the Bible in those little half-hour Bible studies than at any other time in my Christian faith. In time, I felt comfortable enough with those men to reveal how I indeed was on my Christian walk. For the first time, I could tell them plainly how immature I was. I could say to those men I worked with how I was struggling in my faith. Every Bible group I have been part of since has been compared to that group of men.

  I began to open up about my alcoholism to those men, and with their love, they encouraged me to stay in recovery even if it didn't seem like it was working. That small group of three men had a considerable impact on my life. Two of those men took me to rehab and prayed for me before they dropped me off. They always did everything they could to encourage me after I returned, and I kept in contact with them for a little while after I was discharged. They were open and honest about their struggles, and I began to be open and honest about mine. Even when I was lying, they seemed to accept me still.

Romans 12:10 tells us, *"Love one another with brotherly affection. Outdo one another in showing honor" (ESV)*. Those men loved me, and it was not the only time I have had true Christian brotherly love in a group, but it was the first. My years of lying, cheating and drinking were catching up to me. That morning group became my oasis in a sea of my crap. I am forever thankful for Jesus putting people in my life in my early faith who took an interest in me while I was still walking with alcohol more than Christ.

## 2 FRIEND OF BILL W.

It took almost three years in a 12-step recovery before I achieved long-term sobriety. My Marine Corps career was ruined because of my alcoholism. My stint in a drug and alcohol military rehab on Norfolk Navy base was not helpful to my military career. I could write a book alone just about my experiences in 12-step recovery programs. I will refrain and only bring it up because in the rooms of 12-step recovery is where I found God. A personal relationship with my Lord and Savior was introduced to me by a bunch of former drunks. It was a bunch of drunks that first showed me the love of Christ.

I believe I was an alcoholic right out of the box. From my first taste of alcohol, I was in love, and I wanted to feel that way all the time. At fourteen years old, a friend and I camped out in my backyard, and he brought several bottles of liquor. We waited until dark and began drinking. I do not remember much, but I awoke the following day in my bed. I had almost died of alcohol poisoning. I tried to drink more than my fair share and passed out in a ditch going to a girl's house. When I became unresponsive, my friend flagged someone down and was sent to the hospital to pump my stomach. The embarrassment my parents must have felt! I could not imagine. Even with stern and severe punishments imposed, I secretly couldn't wait to do it again.

I joined the Marine Corps right out of high school. I had finally found something I could belong to and feel proud of belonging to. But I learned quickly the "work hard, play hard" mentality was deep in the Marine culture. I deployed every chance I could, trying to build up a false and ego-driven reputation. My drinking increased, and I began to only associate with people who drank like me. Eventually, I noticed I was drinking way more than anyone else, so I began to isolate my drinking to try to protect my addiction. The funny thing about all addictions is once we know at the bottom of our heart they are unhealthy; we begin to lie and manipulate to protect the addiction we love.

I found and fell in love with a woman who was also a Marine who I thought drank just like me, but it turned out she didn't. We were only married for fourteen months. My first wife gave me an ultimatum to go to inpatient alcohol treatment or face divorce. We had no children, and I chose alcohol over my wife. She made the right decision. My drinking got worse. I always wanted to self-isolate and drink, even though I hated to be alone. Any time off the clock meant a bottle in hand.

I met my second wife on New Year's Eve night in 1999 at a club; she spilled a drink on me and wouldn't hush. I fell in love with her from the first moment I met her. The terrible thing about being an alcoholic was I knew deep down she was too good for me. I cleaned my act up a little to impress her and deem myself worthy of her love, but it didn't take too long for her to find out I had my demons; porn and alcohol were surfacing. They always appear slowly, like the frog sitting in a pot with the heat turning up. By the time you know what you got yourself into, it's too late. We were married and had our first child before I believe she knew what I was.

In the *Big Book of 12-Step Recovery*, Co-Founder Dr. Bob states, *"For some reason, we alcoholics seem to have the gift of picking out the world's finest women."* [3] I know we took a vow

---

[3] Bill W., Aaron Cohen, and Bill W., Alcoholics Anonymous: the Original Big Book, 12 Steps, Guides, and Prayers, the Story of How Many Thousands of Men and Women Have Recovered from Alcoholism (Twelve Step Study Guides

for good times and bad, but the lying drunkenness and mayhem she endured for almost five years is enough pain for three lifetimes. I showed up drunk when my daughter was born; I knew what I was doing was wrong. The phenomenon of craving had become almost unbearable. I woke up, and all I thought about was that drink; nothing else mattered. If you are not an addict or alcoholic, you cannot understand the depth of the craving. I always felt it in what seemed like the center of my brain. It was maddening.

With all his wisdom, King Solomon knew this and was puzzled by alcoholism as he stated in *Proverbs 23:29-35 (NIV)*:

*Who has woe? Who has sorrow?*
  *Who has strife? Who has complaints?*
  *Who has needless bruises? Who has bloodshot eyes?*
*Those who linger over wine*
  *who go to sample bowls of mixed wine.*
*Do not gaze at wine when it is red*
  *when it sparkles in the cup,*
  *when it goes down smoothly!*
*In the end, it bites like a snake*
  *and poisons like a viper.*
*Your eyes will see strange sights,*
  *and your mind will imagine confusing things.*
*You will be like one sleeping on the high seas,*
  *lying on top of the rigging.*
*'They hit me,' you will say, 'but I'm not hurt!*
  *They beat me, but I don't feel it!*
*When will I wake up*
  *so I can find another drink?'*

After my daughter's birth, my alcoholism did not just affect my ex-wife and me. My ex-wife took on a more serious approach to my deviant behavior; she is why I

---

Publishing, 2015).

went to my first AA meeting. She found the place. All I had to do was show up. Every addict knows when to play nice to protect their one true love…the addiction they are protecting. I had no intention of doing anything to sober up. I wanted to stop, but the desire to facilitate any real change just wasn't there. I saw what it was doing to those I loved, and I knew alcohol was destroying my family. It is easy to say if you loved them, you would stop. I asked myself that same question all the time; I needed power outside of myself.

I loved my family very much, but I also loved King Alcohol; he ruled me, and I submitted to his will. I would spend hours away from my daughter and ex-wife, claiming I was fishing, but I was drinking instead. I was still going to recovery meetings and felt awful because I simply wasn't getting it. I had spurts when I tried to work the recovery program, and I wasn't getting any better. Like a man crawling uphill in the mud, I wasn't going anywhere but making a mess. I would slip back into desolation, and each time it got worse. I would go to meetings drunk, pass out in the meeting, and wake up only to drive home drunk. I was driving intoxicated everywhere and even sometimes would drive my daughter and ex-wife around drunk.

My ex-wife was never sure when she saw me what state I would be in: drunk or angry. After working all night, I would drink the day away until she came home. One time, I ran out of alcohol and had to go to the store to buy more beer. My foot accidentally slipped off the clutch and hit the accelerator in my drunken stupor, and I hit the vehicle in front of me on my way home. It was a minor fender bender by any account. But the driver of the other vehicle immediately knew I was drinking and called the police. I was in handcuffs within a half-hour, but not before my ex-wife drove by to see me getting handcuffs on. She bailed me out —I had blown three times over the legal limit. The shame I felt was the worst I had felt up to that point in my life. For the first time in my life, I seriously contemplated suicide. I still did not call out to God.

My DUI charge and conviction put a significant strain on my family financially and emotionally. I had more than once drank up all our money, and we had to live quite lean until I got paid again. I frequented a local, poorly-run watering hole because I wanted to hide out with people who wouldn't care. Every morning, I drove to work hungover or still a little drunk, swearing to myself I would not drink that day. I made bargains. I started to pray but had become convinced that God was not listening.

Shortly after finding Jesus that day in church, I regularly attended the woodpile group in Newport, North Carolina. I had a sponsor and also another one. I did everything they suggested when it was convenient and when it served me best at that moment. I cleaned up my outside for appearances after converting, but genuine honesty and humility, the basic recipe of any actual change, escaped me. I was still trying to protect my true love, alcohol. I would go to any length to have my alcohol and maintain my pretentious, newfound Christian faith. It gave my ex-wife false hope, and with my daughter getting older, the divide between us got bigger and bigger. There were people I saw in the programs of recovery coming into the rooms after I did, and their lives were getting truly better. You could see the glow of real growth and happiness in their faces; the recovery program was working. I was still secretly hiding alcohol all over the house, sneaking out to dive bars, and going to meetings with alcohol on my breath.

I had buckled down at one point and decided I would follow the "suggestions" of recovery. I had gotten a sponsor; he was two years sober and also a former Marine. This man tried so hard to help me. He was blunt and loving at the same time. He was available 24 hours a day and 7 days a week; he would answer if I called. He told me if I ever thought about drinking to call him. I tested that theory, so I purchased a bottle, went to my usual drinking place, poured the glass, and then called him and told him what I was planning on doing. His response infuriated me: "Enjoy the drunk. Call me tomorrow if you are serious about staying sober." I got good and drunk on him that night; he knew I had already decided to get drunk. I had bought the booze and found a place—even poured it out. There was no talking me out of it; I was being dramatic and wasting his time. I started over the next day but only tried enough to make it look like I was trying. I ran that poor man ragged. He fired me and told me I was not serious about staying sober and that he wouldn't help me any longer until I was serious.

When I went home and told my ex-wife, she was livid. I played the victim, of course. She called him, and his words to her were harsh but some of the most loving words he could say. He told her I wasn't ready to get sober and that she should protect herself and our daughter from me until I was ready to stop drinking. I shrugged his comments off, but I knew they had a profound impact on her and me. I knew he was right, and I respected him. I still didn't get it.

I loved my daughter deeply, but I would drink with her when I had her alone while she was in my care. I would drive her around drunk. I am humiliated even to this day for my behavior in many ways. It is part of my story; one cannot talk of the light unless he speaks of the dark. My ex-wife caught me drinking with my daughter one last time, and she was a military spouse long enough to know the one person who could make me jump. She contacted the chaplain. The chaplain summoned me and didn't care what I had to say. I immediately knew he had done this before, and he was blunt and forward. He told me to volunteer for inpatient alcohol treatment that day. My military career was hanging on by a thread. Like any good alcoholic, I knew when I was cornered and got honest, just enough to save my skin and protect my addictions as best I could. I went straight to my Command and told them I had a problem, which wasn't hard because they knew I was an alcoholic, but I wasn't exactly ready to do anything about it until forced. They made the arrangements for me to take a trip to Norfolk Navy base for inpatient alcohol treatment.

Many of those men were my friends for many years, and we had been on many deployments together worldwide. I saw this as an opportunity and was willing. I knew alcohol was killing me and hurting my ex-wife and child, and despite my actions to the contrary, I loved them very much. I was drinking not because I wanted to; I drank because I had to. Drinking had ceased being fun years ago. They escorted me to Norfolk Navy base to attend a twenty-eight-day inpatient program. Two close friends were there to make sure I got there sober. I was given a breathalyzer upon entering and thus began one of the most unique experiences of my life.

On my first day, I was amazed at the uniforms' variations—everything from an Army Lieutenant Colonel to Coast Guard Seamen. I began the processing as I was waiting for my turn to meet my counselors. There was a sign in front of me. It was a burned-out lightbulb, and it said, "People don't change because they see the light; they change because they feel the heat." I kept staring at it and trying to place the significance in my own life. I wanted to change and was feeling the heat.

I believe God had that sign placed in my view because I saw the little miracles God was performing in my life. Once I met my counselor, I told that man everything: all the lies, the sneaking around, the driving my daughter around drunk. I poured my guts out to a man I just met, but he seemed unfazed. He only asked me one question: Are you willing to go to any length to get sober? I said yes. He then presented me with a simple marble I still have today. He proclaimed I probably need a marble after all the ones I have lost. After everyone in my group got interviewed, our counselor introduced himself. He was a retired Navy Chief with over twenty-five years in the Navy and twenty years sober in 12-step recovery. He was a slender man and adorned with a leather fanny pack. My group comprised two army soldiers, three sailors, an Airforce Major, and a Marine.

We were kept extremely busy from sunup to sundown, with classes, recovery meetings, one-on-one counseling sessions, and tons of reading and writing assignments. Not a moment was wasted. It was the most challenging academic endeavor I have ever taken on. College and grad school paled in comparison. They kept the standards high. My counselor was the hardest one there amongst the groups. Our one-on-one sessions were emotionally draining. I am convinced he could read my mind. He was never cruel, but he was blunt and forthright. For example, he asked me once to see my daughter's picture; I pulled one out of my wallet and showed him proudly. He grasped the picture, looked at her intensely, looked at me, and then proclaimed that she was a pretty girl. I said, "Yes, she is." His face changed to seriousness. Then he looked at me directly in the eye and said, "Do you want her to grow up to be a loser like you and drive her kid around drunk? "I knew he was right. He then told me it was up to me to break the cycle of addiction in my family.

My counselor in rehab was one of the most influential people in my life. I was just another one of his patients, and he probably never realized the impact he had on me. He was not loving but loved enough to start the hard conversations and say things that upset me, and he never wavered. I believe I owe my life to him. And as the years passed, he has said nothing that didn't end up being true. All the people in my group arrived at different times. Every week, new people came and people left. The following week, we got two new additions to our group.

Justin was a captain in the army; he was loud and outgoing. Everyone seemed to be drawn to him immediately. He seemed to be so full of life; he ended up being the most troubled man I have ever known. There was also one older civilian gentleman amongst new arrivals; he was in rough shape. He was as yellow as a road sign and could not speak. We all helped him to bed in our quad. He had a bracelet and the usual markings of one who just left the hospital. We took turns watching him throughout the night. In the morning, I was to report directly to my counselor's office, which was unusual. I reported in and in the office was also the commanding officer of the Navy rehab facility. It was explained to me who the man was—Harold Castle, an Army retiree who had been kicked out of just about every alcohol rehab facility that the defense department had. He was in the latter stages of alcoholism and delivered to them in the middle of alcoholic seizures. As they were telling me this, I was puzzled why they were telling me this. Then I was rudely enlightened. It was my responsibility to care for him.

On my second week of 28-day alcohol rehab, I was finally starting to think clearly and stopped shaking myself to sleep each night. Struggling under the course load as it was, I began to get my rhythm and make real strides in self-discovery.

Hopeful that I could return home a new man and repair the damage I had caused my family and maybe fix my military career, I thought of the severe effects this would have on me and what I thought was my last chance to improve myself. I lost all military protocol and questioned why the commanding officer was blunt and direct. His response was simple: "Because you're a Marine, and this is what Marines do. Any questions? "I quickly snapped back into the military bearing with a loud, direct "Aye-Aye, sir." My counselor voiced his displeasure at my selfishness to not be overjoyed to help my fellow man. I was to sleep next to him and be with him 24/7, making sure I helped him with anything he needed, with emphasis on anything.

To say that I was displeased would be an understatement; I went to find my new patient. I found him in the bathroom, trying to get his pants up after he had urinated all over himself. I helped him get his urine-soaked pants up and helped him with our schedule. He couldn't speak, which made communication extremely difficult, and he needed help with everything from feeding himself to even wiping himself. I was in the Marine Corps for over twelve years at that point. I found myself at a drug and alcohol rehab and reduced to a wet nurse for an elderly drunk. I grew to hate him. I saw him as a barrier to my recovery. I was only given one shot at recovery, and it was blown, wiping an older man's butt.

Each day got better with him. He began to lift himself out of the fog; within a few days, he could speak again, but that was not exactly a blessing. He had the worst attitude. He swore so much it made his language almost incomprehensible; it was clear he hated everything and everyone. I was convinced the devil himself sent him to sabotage my recovery and everyone else's. He was convinced the FBI wiretapped the building, and the government was after him because of something he uncovered in Vietnam, but he would never tell us what. Sundays were usually our easy days, and I spent the day catching up on uniform preparations and assignments I had been too busy catering to Harold to do. I quickly realized Harold did not wear underwear, and I also discovered he didn't wipe too well. He only had two sets of clothes, and so I was constantly doing his laundry.

I was scrubbing his poop-stained jeans and just lost it; I cried so much the frustration and anger overtook me, and I was left helpless. I had what I believe was a moment of clarity. I knew at that moment why I was taking care of Harold. It wasn't him whom I was caring for, but my future self. His condition was as I was going to end up if I continued to drink as I had. It was an opportunity wrapped in crap-stained jeans. I was wasting it being angry at him. I still hated Harold, but he was tolerable now. Eventually, we became friends. The last week I was in rehab, I had just a few days to go. Harold snuck some beers from the Base Exchange and was caught during our standard breathalyzers. He was immediately kicked out of rehab and was gone within an hour; we exchanged phone numbers. I couldn't help but feel all that was for nothing. He didn't even make it until the end.

A couple of weeks after I got out of rehab, I spoke to Harold for the last time. I called him one night after a meeting to tell him I was thinking about him. Harold was always resistant to the recovery meetings. He felt they always pushed God too much. We all tried to encourage him to be open-minded. But any mention of God, he just clammed up. Even the more palatable Higher Power talk made any spiritual discussion impassable. I had called him several times after rehab to check in with him, and I missed him. There was something about that particular time I called him, and he was drunk as he always was.

He kept telling me he would send me a book called *Soulful Sobriety;* it was recovery without all that "Jesus crap." I knew him well enough to know when he was full of it. His voice sounded strained, and he sounded fatigued, and I suspected his days were numbered. I told him how much he meant to me and wished he would try the meetings again. He dismissed me as he always did, and we said our goodbyes. A week later, I tried to call him, and it just kept ringing. I called again a few weeks later, and the phone was disconnected.

I found his obituary on the internet. His obituary didn't paint the picture of the man I knew. The Harold I knew was a scared kid, just like me in a big kid body. He was my friend, and I miss him even today. I am grateful I met him. I never really told anyone how much Harold meant to me. I still think of him often, and I believe he was a big part of my recovery.

After rehab, I initially went to meetings with enthusiasm but never was entirely willing to do whatever was necessary to maintain my sobriety. After an intense rehab stay, I got a little arrogant and let it slip slowly. I started going to fewer and fewer meetings and put less effort into maintaining and establishing recovery relationships. It was a poison that dripped slowly in my veins and has killed more alcoholics than Jim Beam. It's called complacency, mixed with an undertone of arrogance. I was drunk in my mind but sober, and people in the rooms told me to tread lightly, but I didn't listen. I heard them, but I didn't heed their warnings.

My countless number of relapses always started with just one beer! They ever grew after that with different intensity levels. Sometimes I started out full throttle. Other times, I'd ease into it over several weeks, steadily increasing my alcohol consumption. Each relapse was filled with self-justification, the entire time mitigating my actions too, most significantly, myself. I remember this one relapse, slipping in an occasional beer on the way home from a meeting until I skipped the meetings entirely. I felt justified in my actions. King Alcohol was my savior, deliverer, and my demise, and I knew it. It is pretty perplexing to love something that you know is killing you. In there lies the insanity of alcoholism, and one could write volumes about its gripping effects.

My ex-wife had been around me and my alcoholism enough to see through my lies and know that I hadn't changed who I was. She was justifiably emotionally checked out. With my discharge from the Marine Corps fast approaching, she began to formulate her escape. She moved home to Gaffney, South Carolina. I was powerless to change what I knew was coming. I knew alcohol was destroying my family, and I couldn't stop drinking even for one day; Lord Alcohol had me in his paws. I increasingly felt distant in the meetings I attended. I knew if I were to lose my ex-wife and now two-year-old daughter, I would be dead soon. I would have no reason to stay sober. I would just drink myself into oblivion. For several months, I was in a state of despair.

On August 9, 2005, I had been drinking all morning, and I had been watching the Left Behind series with Kirk Cameron. I fell on my hands and knees in the shower and asked Jesus to help me. I felt him touch me for one of the first times in my life, and it felt good. I finished getting ready and cleaning up the house for my ex-wife's arrival home from work. She knew I had been drinking all morning but decided, as usual, not to rock the drunken boat. I went to a meeting that night and didn't drink and continued not to drink one day at a time. I began to work the program as suggested but continued to not build on relationships in recovery. I was a regular part of the local recovery meeting. My health improved, and my relationship was improving with my ex-wife. I remember how taking my daughter trick-or-treating was joyous that year. I knew she was reasonably pessimistic. She had moments of sobriety with me before, and they always ended the same way. She grew increasingly excited about moving back home, and I was not sure those plans involved me. I began another slow relapse, sneaking drinks in here and there. I am sure she knew and, if not, suspected enough to decide already what to do.

My ex-wife and my daughter moved back to her hometown in the first week of December 2005. We loaded them up, and I remember how excited my daughter was. After I moved them into the home we purchased in Gaffney, I went back to Havelock, North Carolina, to finish up my service obligation. I spent about a week not drinking, then with a vengeance, my drinking resumed. I began a bender for three days that should have killed me. I was drunk all day and every day. Since I was leaving the service and not useful, I came and went as I pleased, and I was positive they were just marking time until I was no longer their problem.

On December 19, 2005, I had one obligation to get my commanding officer's approval for the discharge. I was to be there at 9 a.m. I stopped drinking the night before at a decent time, or so I thought, but after a three-day bender, much was probably still coming out of my pores. I didn't drink that morning. When I showed up that morning sober, he looked at me and said, "You have been drinking again, Rick." He signed my paper with disgust and told me to leave. I had known this man my entire career, and I deployed with him to several not-so-glamorous places. I always respected him, and he did his best to help me. I remember right after I returned from my stint in rehab, he sat me down in his office and told me he believed I was a Marine of the highest caliber as one man talks to another. Still, I was sick and needed to get better, and he would do his best to keep me until I got better.

To say his words were crushing would be an understatement. It wasn't just because he was my commanding officer. He was a man I knew very well, and I trusted him. I became scared not just about dying drunk but living drunk. With the Marine Corps' comforting blanket quickly diminishing, I was undoubtedly at a crossroads. The insanity of alcoholism is not the crazy things you do when you are drinking. Everyone does silly things intoxicated. The absolute insanity is to consume something despite real negative consequences you know are killing you. Alcohol has stripped me of everything I once held very dear: my job, daughter, wife, my self-worth, my health, and I had even begun to see things that weren't there and hear things in my head.

    I was alone in my trailer in Havelock, North Carolina. I had been alone for several weeks to tie up some things before I got out of the service. I had been going to AA meetings for several years now and could unfortunately only summon up a couple of months of sobriety before drinking again. I had been sober for several months since the previous August, yet my ex-wife and daughter had gone. I was growing increasingly suicidal; I talked to my ex-wife on the phone and didn't say so, but she knew I had been drinking again. Once I got discharged a few days later, I wasn't exactly sure where I would go. My ex-wife and I purchased a home in Gaffney, but it wasn't clear when I showed up if I would be allowed in. It was around 10 p.m. I was alone and had been drinking all day after coming back from talking to my commanding officer. Thrust to utter desperation with no reservation, a hurt I wouldn't feel until many years later. I got on my knees and kept pleading with a tear-soaked body to Jesus, help me, please. I said it over and over again. I was crying a deep cry until I slept a full night's sleep, which had been a long time since I had, after crying all night to Jesus just to help me with no reservation in my heart. I got up that next morning and cleaned the place up, emptied all the alcohol bottles. I saw no angels, Charlton Heston, or a burning bush. But I haven't had a drink since that day; my sobriety date is December 20, 2005.

## 3 KEEP COMING BACK

I took care of what was needed and left the service sober; I had a feeling like I was protected and left the service without incident. I drove to where my family was, knowing it would be okay but unsure if I would be allowed in the door. I remember feeling protected the whole drive to Gaffney. I pulled into our home and knocked on the door, and I remember my ex-wife answered the door and didn't open it completely until after she thoroughly looked me over to ensure I was sober. She was at a crossroads, and she let me in. I do sometimes think that she made the wrong decision. I immediately, and with enthusiasm, grasped the program of recovery. I had been to that recovery group while visiting Gaffney and even used to go to the meetings after sneaking a few drinks in some of Gaffney's finest establishments. I fully embraced the program as I never had before; I went to every meeting I could. My new life revolved around recovery; I lived meeting to meeting. It wasn't easy; the temptation was with me daily, and in some moments, I had to say the serenity prayer over and over to make it home. The mantra of a day at a time was sometimes fifteen minutes at a time.

To secure the mortgage on our house, I had to have a job immediately after leaving the service. I didn't have a plethora of transferable job skills after I left the service. Six months before my end of service, I interviewed with almost a dozen companies with no luck. On a whim and in desperation, I applied to McDonald's as a manager. I was desperate and was shocked when they emailed me back to set up an interview. I traveled to Gaffney for the interview and was hired. Thus began the most important and meaningful job of my life. I started two days after I left the service; I was only sober for like a week out of the Marine Corps after over twelve years. A perfect time as any to peddle some hamburgers!

I learned more about myself at that job than in any other position of my life. It taught me something I had yet to learn. True humility. Marines are naturally arrogant, and the natural narcissism necessary for active addiction was a hurdle. So naturally, I believed I was the center of the world. McDonald's fixed that quickly; I was no longer unique, which became frighteningly clear. Nobody cared who I was or what I had done, real or imagined; I was just another dude trying to earn a nickel and survive. For my first couple of weeks, I woke every morning with the shakes from alcohol withdrawal. Many of the days, in the beginning, I just went from one evolution to another. If I could make it to work without drinking, I would be safe until I got off. A couple of hours before my shift ended, I would become fearful whether I could make it home. Once my shift was up, if I could make it home without drinking, I would be safe. I would usually call my sponsor or someone in the program to tide me over until the meeting that night; this routine went on for months.

I would read my Bible or recovery literature every chance I could with such passages as Galatians 6:8. I continuously repeated when in distress, *"Whoever sows to please their flesh, from the flesh will reap destruction; whoever sows to please the Spirit, from the Spirit will reap eternal life" (NIV)*. I desperately didn't want to drink anymore, but my mind and body would continuously try to trick me because my addiction played havoc in my head. I can only thank Jesus for giving me the strength to endure. I don't understand how I could hold out when the temptation was that strong. The weeks turned into months. To say I hated that job at the beginning would be an understatement. However, as the months ticked by and I began to enjoy the by-products of sobriety and correct living, I still hated the job, but I became grateful for it because it was our only income for a good while. McDonald's was good to my family and me; they gave me a job when I needed it most, put food on our table, and kept the roof over our heads. I will be forever grateful to them.

My daughter, after I sobered up, was the only person who liked me. Being an active alcoholic is a surefire way to isolate yourself from those closest to you. My ex-wife loved me but rightly hated my guts, and I believe everyone else was the same. I was sober and trying to live right, but I think everyone held the "wait and see" mentality with me and justifiably so. But not my daughter. I fell in love with her, and she loved me back; with me being sober, I showered her with attention and love. I showed up to her birth drunk, and now she was the most central thing in my world. My ex-wife would take her to see me during my lunch break at McDonald's. I would always be ashamed to have them see me in a McDonald's uniform. It wasn't exactly where I saw myself, but looking back, I was right where I was supposed to be.

My daughter was so proud of me for working at McDonald's. I got her all the coolest happy meal toys. She even bragged to her friends at church that her dad worked at McDonald's. They responded with envy as their parents were only doctors and lawyers. Her face always lit up when she saw me at work, and every time she saw me. Over the years, I have tried my best to express how much I love her. I am eternally grateful to her for all she has done for me. My daughter saved me. I doubt I would have stayed sober without her love; we were always close. One of my favorite places has always been right beside her while holding her little hand in mine. I just knew I could keep going. She gave me strength when I didn't have any; she was my little angel. I owe her so much, and I have never forgotten it. It pains me even more, knowing the shame I recently brought her.

My ex-wife was aware of my August 9 sobriety date, but I was not rigorously honest about my last bender.

I even picked up chips marking the time of sobriety from August. With the August yearly anniversary getting close, I knew I had to get honest. I spent several weeks mulling over what I knew I had to do. I had a strong suspicion if I didn't come clean, I wouldn't make a year. One of the first times in my life, I did the right thing even when it was hard. I told my ex-wife, and she knew I drank in December but said nothing. I told all the homegroup members, yet I was received with love and tolerance. I was expecting ridicule and shame. For the first time, I started to believe I could make it to a year without drinking.

My life kept getting better, and more and more opportunities started coming our way; the miracle of recovery was coming true in my life. I left McDonald's and got a job as a production supervisor. Because of my military service and the GI bill, I was fortunate enough to begin college at Limestone College in January 2007. With over a year in recovery, I had worked through all the steps of recovery. In many ways, I had begun to put my life in order. Many were still justifiably skeptical, my ex-wife included. With the new job and everything going well, we tried for another child, and our son Ben was born May 29, 2007. He was a handsome young boy, and I was sober during his delivery, which was a blessing. My daughter was delighted and smitten with him from the start. We even invented a holiday for my daughter, "big sister day," which made her feel special on that day. Of course, this trajectory has changed slightly over the years. God has blessed me with two lovely healthy children.

I still attended meetings quite regularly and was highly active in my homegroup. I had a group of people I had cleaned up with. We all had about the same amount of time, and though our stories were different, they were similar in many ways. We always made it a point to talk to each other on the phone and especially at meetings. I noticed I was the only one of that group who wasn't sponsoring someone. Sponsoring someone and guiding them through the twelve steps of recovery is a huge responsibility. You are their greatest coach through recovery. Just as it says in Galatians 6:1: "Brothers and sisters, if someone is caught in a sin, you who live by the Spirit should restore that person gently" (NIV). The essential requirement to be a sponsor is you have successfully worked the steps and have a sponsor. I met both criteria, and yet nobody had asked me. One selects a sponsor because their recovery looks good on them; someone new wants what you have.

All my friends with similar time clean had folks they were sponsoring, and some had two. I admit I was jealous and self-conscious of those who were carrying the message of recovery. I talked it over with my sponsor, and he told me when the teacher is ready, the student will appear. Well, I wouldn't say I liked that answer, so I began hunting myself a sponsee. I upped my meeting attendance and sat next to all the newcomers hoping one poor fool would ask me. Nothing happened, and as weeks went by, I started to become discouraged, like I exhumed something that wasn't desirable in recovery. One day at a noon meeting in Shelby, I walked past Bob, who I will never forget.

Bob was a short man with an unkempt appearance, and he reeked of alcohol; I sat right next to him. I always enjoyed sitting next to people who came into meetings smelling of alcohol; I would reminisce of when I used to go into meetings stinking of vodka. I thought no one knew I had been drinking, but they all knew. He blurted out in the middle of the recovery meeting that he needed a sponsor, and with me sitting next to him, I strategically positioned myself to land my first sponsee. I was elated beyond measure. I promptly gave him my number without hesitation, and I received his. I gave him specific directions to call me the next day to start work on the steps. I also told him to call me in the meantime if he felt the urge to drink. In my jubilation, I failed to concede the fact he already smelled like a gin mill.

I left the meeting on cloud nine with my new status as a twelve-step recovery sponsor. I began running through my head the scene where he passionately and with tears in his eyes thanked me after I handed him his one year of sobriety coin. I began to map out the step work I was to give him. I was in my head, laying the groundwork for his recovery. I bubbled with purpose and excitement at the opportunity the good Lord had laid at my feet. I would go to any lengths to help him stay sober, all before he even called me. The next twenty-four hours were a fury of anticipation at this blessing. I went to the same meeting the next day with much eagerness to see my new prospect. He was not there as I expected; I began to worry and raced home. I called my sponsor and told him of my new sponsee. He was supportive and counseled that I knew that if he were earnest, he would call. He said those who are serious about a solution will always seek it. I listened politely and began to wait by the phone lest I miss his call. I am a sponsor and can help someone heal from alcoholism.

Despite advice from a man with over thirty years of recovery, I called Bob. He answered the phone, and I began to inquire why he failed to contact me and why he missed the meeting. I don't recall ever hearing his response. Instead, I began preaching recovery to him for almost an hour. I told my recovery journey, quoted the recovery literature, and shared my experience, strength, and hope with him until I was blue in the face. I was going to make him believe he needed to be sober, and of course, I alone was the only one duly qualified to help him. He listed intently. I could hear a fridge door open several times. Still, I paid no attention to it since such an insignificant fact didn't play into the narrative of soul-saving I found myself currently occupying. I am working on Bob with all the fervor of a preacher at an old-fashioned tent revival. After I talked myself out, I made him promise to call me tomorrow or if he felt like drinking, day or night. I encouraged him to go to the same noon meeting where I first saw him; he promised to do everything I asked.

The next day he didn't show to the meeting, and he failed to call me, and thus the routine began; I started to pay more and more attention to the sound of the fridge door opening. After several rotations, I started to lose my resolve and finally asked Bob if he was even interested in getting sober. He politely said no. He only needed a telephone number of a contact to give to the Alcohol and Drug Policy Commission to show that he attended a twelve-step recovery meeting. It finally dawned on me he was drinking beer the entire time I was "preaching" to him. In an instant, the man I so desperately wanted to deliver from the gates of alcoholism smashed the ego-fueled hopes of being the "Billy Graham" of recovery were squandered instantly. He thanked me very much for my concern and said that he appreciated the talks. Bob was a polite, pleasant man. I became enraged with bitterness because my sponsor was right, and I went against his better judgment and chased Bob. This experience would prove to be a valuable lesson in the years to come. Even Jesus said in Matthew 10:14, *"If anyone will not welcome you or listen to your words, leave that home or town and shake the dust off your feet" (NIV)*.

A couple of months later, after I quit looking to fix someone, someone asked me to help them. Over the next couple of years, I sponsored several dozen men from different backgrounds and socioeconomic statuses. Addiction doesn't care who you are or where you are from, it is the ultimate equalizer, and it is a rapacious creditor. Addiction touches everyone from septic tank repairers who drank only beer to a director of a Sunday school at a local Baptist church who loved to buy a bunch of crack cocaine for strippers and make the family bank account melt like snow in June. Addiction doesn't care; it renders all to their core. None of them stayed clean; they all eventually went back to drinking and drugging. Suppose I would voice my grievance to any brothers in recovery over my lack of ability to help anyone truly. They were always quick to point out I was still sober, which was the most crucial fact. It would comfort me minimally because I genuinely wanted to change someone's life for the better. In my mind, I was merely taking the pain away for a bit. I know now my disparity fed my other addiction.

    I became involved in-service work with recovery and became the local representative of my group. On one occasion, my ex-wife and I went to a Recovery Conference for Alcoholism. I made the hotel reservation through that organization. And when I checked in, they gave me two free tokens for cocktails at the bar once we checked in. I questioned the women why they were handing them out. She replied it was customary for all significant conferences booked at that hotel. I reminded the lady it was a conference for recovering alcoholics. She stated she had handed them out to all the people who checked into that conference; we both had a good laugh over that. She was very embarrassed, but I assured her it was fine. The following day, I kept my tokens in fear of a token count. As my time in recovery grew, I no longer feared getting drunk. I kept doing what I knew had worked. I went to several meetings a week, became involved, and made recovery a priority. I kept church attendance up and was trying to grow spiritually. I graduated from college and graduate school with degrees in accounting; recovery afforded me a clear head to do such a thing. I landed a job as an accountant shortly after graduating from graduate school. The miracle of recovery was happening in my life; my recovered life was better than I could have imagined.

A few months later, I would meet a man that would have a massive impact on my life. I went to the Saturday noon meeting as I usually did, and in the meeting, two men had just been released from prison and were not wanting to go back out to drinking and using. They were both genuine and seemed sincere. Plus, they were both on parole and were eager to turn their lives around. They attended every meeting they could; neither one of them had licenses or vehicles. I, among many others, picked them up to go to a meeting and dropped them off. One of them asked me to sponsor him within a few days. Picking people up and dropping them off from meetings was always overly burdensome and problematic to the family, but I could not escape the simple phrase, "What would thy maker wish!"

To combine time and help those two get to more meetings, I began taking them early Sunday morning before church and Sunday school. Early morning meetings were always good meetings because those who curtailed sleeping to make a meeting were usually very serious about their recovery.

They were both willing to get up very early on a Sunday morning for a meeting. I woke up before everyone else to pick them up and drive the twenty miles to the meeting; I met my family at church and even made my men's Sunday school class. If I hurried, I'd only be ten minutes late. I had gotten grief over the years because of my absence at church events while attending recovery meetings, but it never bothered me too much. It was simply because they were not addicts and understood nothing about recovery. A few weeks showing up late, I started hearing vocal complaints of my tardiness, little sly comments disguised as a jest, but it was apparent their undertone. A verbal proclamation to the whole class of, "I am sorry I was late. I've been working with these two young men to help them stay sober by taking them to a meeting in (town twenty miles away) at 7 a.m. Both just got out of prison and didn't have vehicles. I try my best not to be late" shut up most. One particular obnoxious deacon only dug his heels in more rigid and even went as far as asking me what was more critical, "recovery or Jesus." I wanted to slap his ignorant smug look off his face but refrained and then told him I was picking him up the following Sunday at 7 a.m. sharp. And if he weren't out front, I would come into his house and get him. I didn't take no for an answer. I reassured him Jesus knows exactly where he was going and that he would be attending the meeting with us.

    The following Sunday, I was promptly at that man's home at the agreed-on time, and he was waiting out front. We talked, and he was pleasant and confessed he was a little excited and nervous, also that he knew nothing about 12-step meetings. We were to pick up my usual two, and we had one more I was picking up. The additional man lived in the Gaffney area known as "Happy Valley," and I can assure you the deacon was not happy when I informed him where we were going first. I had already told the men I was picking up that there we would be someone else. I asked them to be polite and encouraged them to openly talk about any prison stories they would like to share during the ride to the meeting. We arranged the seating in my ex-wife's van, so our guest was seated in the middle of my two regulars. They were both somewhat muscular men in their thirties. I checked on him periodically in the rear-view mirror. I could tell he was uncomfortable, and this was a Sunday like no other for him. He was huddled between two muscular felons trading prison stories on the way to a recovery meeting.

Once we got to the meeting, I walked in with him. It was apparent he felt more relaxed. One thing I have always noticed about recovery meetings, it is a melting pot. I have sat next to lawyers on one side and former prostitutes who teach Sunday school on the other. Nobody cares anything about you except for one fact: that you genuinely desire to get clean. I have met thousands of people in recovery, and I rarely ever find out anything outside the rooms is essential. Even among my best friends in recovery today, I do not know who they vote for, their religion, who their family is or isn't. I could talk for hours and only talk about what truly binds us all together to stay clean, help others, and truly connect to who we choose to call God. It is, in many ways, more of a Christian tool than several churches I have attended. After the meeting, he thanked me before we piled in the van. He described it as enlightening and said it wasn't what he thought it was going to be. He never hassled me again for being late to Sunday school; neither did anyone else.

I continued to sponsor that man; the days ticked into weeks and months. We were becoming real friends; he shared some of the most intimate details of his life as I walked him through the steps, and I shared some of mine. It was a relationship built on trust and respect. His life began to get better; he secured a fine job and was ecstatic. With his first paycheck, he bought a used moped. When he called me and told me about his purchase, he told me how great God was and how grateful he was for the gift of sobriety. I was thankful as it eased the burden of picking him and dropping him off several times a week. He began to take more mentoring roles in the meetings, leading the meetings and encouraging new arrivals. I was incredibly proud of the Godly man he was becoming.

I had gotten a new job as a staff accountant at a local plant, and as is customary, your boss takes you to lunch. My new boss made me well aware of his church resume, and I spent the hour-long lunch listening to him brag about his Christian resume. He told me about all the mission trips he went on and how he struggled to run the finest choir in all the south that would be in chaos without his gifts and talents. Plus, he told me of his awards and vast recognitions in his church community. He had graduated from Clemson University and made that point very clear of how blessed he was to get such a superior education. I tried my best to exercise my listening skills and saw it as an opportunity to show some humility. But I admit I was thinking I made the wrong decision taking the job.

Several months went by when my sponsee would only call me out of his regular times if something were wrong. I have always been open about my recovery. Hence, every place I have worked knew I was in recovery and occasionally got personal calls from others trying to stay sober. My sponsee called me about one in the afternoon and told me that his moped would not start and that he wouldn't be able to make it to work that day, plus he wasn't sure he had enough money to repair it. He was frustrated; his life had been ticking along, getting better with minimal bumps. But if he couldn't get to work, they would fire him, and they took a chance on hiring a convicted felon; it was tough to get a decent job, and he didn't know if he could get one again. He talked his way through the problem. Then he told me with the sincerity of a thousand preachers, "I know God has got my back, and this is going to work out. I will pray His will be done, then try to find someone to fix the moped. I will work something with the money." I was impressed with his faith. We had several dozen conversations like that throughout our relationship, but what made this one stick out is what happened next.

I went to my desk to work and noticed my boss

was more distant than usual, but I didn't pry. About 3 p.m., he called me into his office and informed me he was let go because of his performance. During the next hour, he began telling me all the details of his mistreatment and a big mistake the company was making. He informed me of his compensation to stay on for the next four months to train his replacement. He was being compensated one year of his annual salary as severance to stay on for the four months; I was the staff accountant and was thus privy to a lot of information. I knew his annual salary was over ninety thousand dollars a year. As he told me this grave news, I failed to see the downside; it seemed like an inconvenient blessing. I tried to console him as best I could, but sometimes people, including myself, need to whine a bit. I could not fail to see the irony before me, which bore a lesson I still carry to this day.

With his extensive religious resume and because of pride and emotionalism, my boss failed to see the opportunities to be grateful. The man I was sponsoring with his problems seemed at face value more severe, but he didn't fail to realize that God was going to look after him as long as he did the right thing. That night I took him and his moped to a "repairman" that was the dope dealer he used when he was actively using. The drug dealing repairman worked out a payment plan with him. He didn't want to be there alone; I stayed with him at the dope house until the dope-man completely fixed his moped. Despite urging from the repairman, he asked if we needed "anything else." We both knew what that meant, and I was glad I could be there for him. We sat on the tailgate of my truck, sipping Mountain Dews until late in the night, talking about recovery and faith. I shared my boss's problems with him and his reaction; we both had a hardy laugh about it. I never forgot the lessons of that day and hoped I never would. I guess Jesus was right when he said in Matthew 20:16, *"So the last shall be first, and the first last: for many be called, but few chosen" (NIV).*

The twelve steps of recovery are a pathway to get your life together and a direction to find God in working with him. I shared my faith with him, and steps two and three deal specifically with God or a Higher Power. Step two says, "We came to believe that a Power greater than ourselves could restore us to sanity." And step three, "Make a decision to turn our will and our lives over to the care of God as we understood Him." In working through these steps with him, I encouraged him to reach out to religious organizations; he was resistant at first. He would find many things before they were officially deemed lost in his active addiction to support his drug habit. He stole everything to support his addiction. He became interested in the church where his mother attended, with whom he was extremely close to. She was in this church every time the doors were open. Upon my encouragement, he attended the church of his youth with his mother; it was only several months since his release from jail, and he had stolen from quite a few people in that congregation. After the preacher's service, he was asked politely not to attend anymore by the Preacher, at least not now since the wounds of his misgivings in that church were still a little too raw. He was upset at first, but mostly because it embarrassed his mother. I called the preacher the following Monday and asked him to reconsider, which he wouldn't. Astonishingly, my sponsee was not too sore at the congregation because he secretly confessed to me he had stolen from that preacher. With honesty, we can paint the whole picture. I was more upset than he was. After all, I wanted him to stay clean because I knew him to be a good man despite his gruff immature exterior, and he was my friend.

# 4 HOPE FOR CHEROKEE

In a church organization, there is the pastor and maybe deacons, Sunday school teachers, youth leaders, etc. In recovery, the founders of recovery wanted to keep the organization minimum; I can only assume to encourage hierarchies' natural ability to establish themselves based on competence. Naturally, competence in anything; may be given with positional authority, but that isn't always the case. In recovery, time spent clean and sober should reflect an appropriate level of competence in recovery as with anything that isn't necessarily the case. At different times in my recovery, I haven't always reflected a spiritual aptitude as one should expect. Time sober doesn't equate to recovery wisdom, just as church attendance doesn't liken one to a stronger relationship with Jesus.

With experience, it doesn't always equate to wisdom; there are old fools and young ones. Several of the more senior members began critiquing the members with less "time" in recovery beyond patient, loving correction. The members started grumbling, and that man I was sponsoring was chief among the grumblers. I did my best to guide it constructively. There was no specific recovery program for drug addiction. Much of the older members' critiques that the newer members were about them openly sharing their stories and mentioning drug addiction in a recovery program centered on alcoholism. The mere mention of them saying they were recovering drug addicts versus recovering alcoholics would invite ridicule from the "bleeding deacons."

Tensions had boiled over enough, and several men got together to form a drug addiction twelve-step group in Cherokee county. I count myself blessed to be among that group, and of the six men that met that

Saturday afternoon, only three are still in recovery, and one of them is dead. My sponsor and I were the only ones with over a year clean. It was my sponsee's idea to start the group, and a former teacher did most of the heavy lifting to get the meeting started. I have heard it said many times in recovery that to create a new recovery group, all you need is "resentment and a coffee pot," and it chimed true. I was immensely proud of those men who were incarcerated by the state just a short time ago and were now forming a recovery group for drug addiction.

After they invited the other local groups to attend in the area, they decided on a name, came up with "Hope for Cherokee," and set a date for their first meeting. The first meeting was on a Sunday night, and there were over twenty people in recovery there; everyone was grateful for starting the meeting. Many of us were not expecting such a strong turnout at the first meeting, and the second meeting was even more robust. I can see the beaming of pride and elations of those responsible for starting the meeting in their faces and body language. It was a big deal and looked very much as though the meeting was there to stay. The irony of that meeting was that it began from resentment; sometimes, the conflict we get in life is God's way of pushing us to something more magical.

Despite his success in the first drug addiction recovery meeting in Cherokee county, my sponsee began to distance himself. After the Saturday noon meeting, I knew something was wrong as I had spent a considerable amount of time with this man for almost a year. I knew his deepest darkest secrets, and he knew mine. I knew something was bothering him so. I pressed him, but not like a brother in Christ should push. I did just enough to put the check-in the block. I left the meeting and went home to my family; knowing something was wrong, I was sure he would tell me later or work it out on his own. I regret that decision even to this day. I took the easy road; I was polite, but I was cowardly.

I heard nothing from him ever again, which was the last I saw of him. That Sunday night, I had gotten a phone call from a friend in recovery, and he had told me. His mother and his best friend returned from a weekend and came home Sunday night to find him dead. He had overdosed on a mixture of different drugs and alcohol. I immediately left to go to his home; along the way, I picked someone else up. His mother, who I knew well, was in shock. I went downstairs to their basement, where his body was when everyone was in front talking. I held his hand; it was not entirely cold yet; I kissed his forehead and told him I loved him. He was my friend, and I still feel responsible for his death. No matter what anyone says, I think I should have pressed him when I knew something was wrong.

I dried my tears and went upstairs, and in that living room smiling was the preacher who had asked him not to show up at his church. I never in my life wanted to slap the face of a man so much as that preacher. He was smiling; he was oblivious to the fact that the dead body sitting in the basement was the body of a man who, just weeks earlier, was denied entrance into his flock. We exchanged formalities, and he recognized me from his phone call. I made it clear in the conversational tone of my annoyance of his presence, but he was not there for him; he was there for his mother. And she was glad he was there, and I cannot be so sure he made the wrong decision. I have always regretted it when I let my spiritual immaturity control me.

I took his death hard; he was the first person in recovery. I let him see the real me entirely. My ex-wife is the only other person. Despite his gruff exterior and the fact we came from entirely different backgrounds, I know he trusted me completely. He shared his innermost thoughts and fears with me, which made me trust him. In recovery, we do a fifth step which is essentially a confession of our deepest, darkest secrets. It is a vital part of the recovery. The Big Book of Alcoholics Anonymous says, *"This is perhaps difficult - especially discussing our defects with another person. We think we have done well enough in admitting these things to ourselves. There is doubt about that. In actual practice, we usually find a solitary self-appraisal insufficient. Many of us thought it necessary to go much further. We will be more reconciled to discussing ourselves with another person when we see good reasons why we should do so. The best reason first: If we skip this vital step, we may not overcome drinking. Time after time, newcomers have tried to keep to themselves certain facts about their lives. Trying to avoid this humbling experience, they have turned to easier methods. Almost invariably, they got drunk. Having persevered with the rest of the program, they wondered why they fell. We think the reason is that they never completed their housecleaning. They took inventory all right but hung on to some of the worst items in stock. They only thought they had lost their egoism and fear; they only thought they had humbled themselves. But they had not learned enough of humility, fearlessness, and honesty; in a sense, we find it necessary until they told someone else all their life story."* [4]

    I gave my most thorough fifth step, I had ever given to that point to him as he gave me his. Trust is a big thing; if we know the person we are talking to trusts us, we are more likely to trust them and be completely open with them. He was the first person I disclosed how much of a grip sexual lust had on me; he never judged me for it, and it was freeing to tell him. I believe a lot of the guilt I still carry for not confronting my sponsee when I knew

---

[4] Bill W., Aaron Cohen, and Bill W., Alcoholics Anonymous: the Original Big Book, 12 Steps, Guides, and Prayers, the Story of How Many Thousands of Men and Women Have Recovered from Alcoholism (Twelve Step Study Guides Publishing, 2015).

something was wrong is because I knew how much he trusted me. I still feel like I betrayed his trust as much as my infidelity with my ex-wife, which I will discuss in great detail in later chapters. He was her only son, and looking back; I didn't grieve well; I regrettably avoided his mother. I knew her well, but my feelings of guilt and shame kept me from consoling her in her loss; I was selfish. I let them both down and hope they can both forgive me.

    The funeral services were held in the same church of which he was refused to attend, ironically. Some men and I from recovery were asked to be pallbearers. There were also some friends from school, one man, in particular; our conversation would forever change my perspective. After some light conversations, he was a schoolmate; he seemed comfortable enough to share his struggle with his friend's death. He had looked at me with a puzzled face, and I could see he was fighting back the tears. He asked me if it made any sense to him dying loaded; he was such a great guy, and it just seemed pointless. I didn't answer him; I just patted him on the back. I thought deeply about this because, at face value, it seemed like his death was pointless. Any addict's death seems pointless as one dies in consumption of pure pleasure; it is the shallowest of deaths, like a dog that dies from sneaking some antifreeze.

    I then began to think some more about it and then thought about the group he helped start. I began to think of the number of people who attended that meeting regularly. I also began to reflect on the lives affected and the Hope for Cherokee group's future lives. On average, they had at least twenty to sometimes forty people hearing the good news about recovery. Suppose you multiply that out over the years, thousands of people whose lives have been affected by opening a proven avenue of recovery to battle addiction and come to know God. Once I started to think of the magnitude and potential impact, by creating just that one meeting. His life didn't seem so inept and void of meaning. I communicated this to his friend from high school; as I was talking, I could see his face brighten as he fully grasped the impact of his life on others. I don't know too many people who can claim to help start something changing lives. I still go to that meeting until this day and know people who have not only stopped using drugs and alcohol but transformed their lives and have found God. Recovery is one of the most beautiful examples of God working through others I have ever seen, and what he started is changing lives.

The smiling preacher gave a eulogy on the casket before him, as best as one could. He didn't know him as I had known him; to him, he was just another drug addict struck down by sin and addiction, and he probably had given at least a dozen or more funerals just like this one. I have met very few preachers that understood addiction. At the end, he mentioned his recovery and what a positive impact it had on his life and his grieving mother; and how thankful he was and mostly his mother for the people in recovery for the last year of his life clean and sober. He professed he would like to attend a meeting to learn of recovery's miracle at the end of the sermon.

My resentment began to fade for the smiling preacher. I saw a providential order to introduce that preacher to recovery, hoping to shed some light on the strictly anonymous program and possibly bring some positives back to his congregation. I decided I was going to invite him to a meeting after the graveside service. After the service, I invited him to a meeting and was immediately told by his mannerism and tone he wasn't interested. I gave him my number and was excited about the possibility, but I am still to this day waiting on his phone call. I must always mean what I say and be willing to follow through with my words; just because of man's title doesn't make him immune to that fact.

I remained active in recovery but didn't sponsor anyone for about a year; my other addiction to pornography began to take off about that time. I was looking to soothe myself and a lot of self-apathy, but I will discuss this at great length in the next chapter. The recovery group I was attending began to get an influx of newcomers while the "old-timers" were leaving and hoping for a Cherokee meeting to provide a place for those suffering from drug addiction. It offered a perfect opportunity for me to be helpful. After about a year hiatus from sponsoring people, I began to sponsor people again. I always feel it is my Christian duty to help those suffering from addiction as I had overcome my addiction through the proven process of twelve-step recovery.

In one area of my addiction, I had all the answers as I was absent from alcohol use and rarely, if ever, got tempted to drink. My other demons began to take shape, and in retrospect, I can see our well-intended paths aren't always the right ones. In the Big Book of Alcoholics Anonymous, "If sex is very troublesome, we throw ourselves harder into helping others." I dove headfirst into trying to help anyone that came into the door. I had sponsored several dozen men over the years, and it was always an emotional roller coaster because you can still see yourselves in others. I remember undoubtedly the pain my alcoholism caused me. Nobody walked into a recovery meeting because their life was going well or acted up in Sunday School. I remember the long walk of shame, walking into your first meeting.

Every person in recovery remembers their first time going to a meeting, the shame and humiliation to go to have a paper signed from a court or the last effort of desperation. I believe because of this, every person in recovery, with little exception, is exceptionally and genuinely welcoming to anyone new in recovery. I still have the meeting schedule from my first meeting with over ten men's home and cell numbers. The tragedy of recovery is only four of the ten men are still clean and sober today. It was customary in most groups I attended that a schedule and all available people from the same sex would jot their telephone number on a schedule and hand them to the new person at the end of the meeting. Despite long periods of many decades of being clean, an overwhelming majority of those in recovery never lose their poverty of spirit with addiction. Poverty brings us the awareness of our fragile recovery. We have always been in the new person's shoes, and we remember.

As it is said in the song by Staind Outside.

*"But I'm on the outside and I'm looking in*
*I can see through you, see your true colors*
*Cause inside you're ugly; you're ugly like me*
*I can see through you, see to the real you."*

I began sponsoring people again and thus began the cycle all over again. Someone would ask for help, and I would sponsor them. I would be at their complete disposal twenty-four hours a day, seven days a week, doing everything I could to help them. They would lose interest in recovery, and I wouldn't hear from them again. I would sponsor another one; their life would get better, and they would not see the point of completing the entire process, and then poof, they were gone. They quit calling, going to meetings, and returning phone calls. I did the same thing repeatedly; I would keep telling myself, and I indeed did the same thing to my sponsors when I first started coming to meetings. Working the twelve steps of recovery is not for the faint of heart; it is time-tested to get your life together and overcome addiction. Most importantly, it is a way to find God. I felt but never admitted to anyone; if I could only get one sponsee to long-term sobriety and get them to sponsor someone else, it would validate myself and justify my efforts all those years.

In many respects, it was not the purest of motives; I wanted to help people, but if I am to be candid, being of service to my fellow man was not the main driving force behind my actions. I was spending more and more time away from home. I would go to any length sometimes to help people get sober even if they were not totally on board with that level of commitment. I had forgotten the lessons learned from Bob and was driven by ego, which in many ways just like the acronym E.G.O (Easing God Out). In my limited experience, anytime an effort is pursued without the purest of motives and isn't aligned with God's will, I lose God's protection in that effort.

To grow, I must continuously put my efforts to the litmus test of motives; I depend on other people's opinions of me. I mask my pursuit to help my fellow alcoholics boost my ego and set myself as the noble martyr. I felt a little bit superior to those good Christian folks, at least in my warped mind in many ways. I used recovery as an excuse not to get involved in my church. I busied myself with what was ego-inflating instead of what was humbling. I was extremely comfortable in recovery and had been clean for a very long time. I know I have never grown to be satisfied; I must push myself to be uncomfortable. Pain is growth, as I have heard many times from my sponsor, but I realize now that pain can be self-initiated by pushing ourselves towards our betterment. Or the latter, which is the pain that is caused by us not aligning our will with God.

I was highly active in my home group and did everything I could to keep those meetings open and flourishing. I welcomed everyone who came; even if our motives are not the purest, it doesn't deflate the endeavor's purity. I have seen addiction destroy families, including my own. All are sorry for him if a person has cancer, and no one is angry or hurt. Still, with addiction, the sickness is just as real as cancer. Still, the almost deliberate destruction of one's family for the consumption of something bewilders all those around the addict that seems practically intentional to everyone except those who have been afflicted by addiction; it's genuinely is baffling. One who has overcome addiction is uniquely equipped to reach out to fellow sufferers because of the many misunderstandings of addiction and the inability of the addict to be completely honest with anyone unless a deep level of trust is solidified through shared experiences. In many ways, addiction is the cancer of our day. It's just like that story I have heard many times, as follows.

Once upon a time, an older man used to go to the ocean to do his writing. He had a habit of walking on the beach every morning before he began his work. Early one morning, he was walking along the shore after a big storm had passed and found the vast beach littered with starfish as far as the eye could see, stretching in both directions.
Off in the distance, the older man noticed a small boy approaching. As the boy walked, he paused every so often, and as he grew closer, the man could see that he was occasionally bending down to pick up an object and throw it into the sea. The boy came closer still, and the man called out, "Good morning! May I ask what it is that you are doing?"

The young boy paused, looked up, and replied, "Throwing starfish into the ocean. The tide has washed them up onto the beach, and they can't return to the sea by themselves," the youth replied. "When the sun gets high, they will die unless I throw them back into the water."
The old man replied, "But there must be tens of thousands of starfish on this beach. I'm afraid you won't really be able to make much of a difference."

The boy bent down, picked up yet another

starfish, and threw it as far as he could into the ocean. Then he turned, smiled, and said, "It made a difference to that one!"

I was increasingly spending less and less time at home and was always on the phone with the people I was sponsoring. I believed I was serving God's will for me, but I was still secretly prideful that those "good Christian folk" could see what impact I was having in the community and what I was doing. My marriage was at the worst it had ever been, yet I spent time with strangers trying to help them get clean. While doing "the Lord's work," I believed I was protected, but I can see now how misguided I was. The newcomers in the meetings began to pressure me to start a newcomer meeting and then began to spend even more time away from home.

Every Friday night for almost three years, I would rush home, argue with my ex-wife about supper and my need to get to the meeting, and then rush off to help drunks who weren't as sincere about staying clean as the effort I was putting in. I wouldn't get home sometimes until late into the night as I was always volunteering to give a perfect stranger a ride home, spend countless time with them after the meeting, sharing my innermost details, and preaching to them about the miracles of recovery. I put great effort into trying to save people and blurring the strict rules of only working with the same sex in recovery, which would prove catastrophic later on. Practices are put in place for good reasons, and when we begin to bend them, at least in my case, it was arrogance in thinking I knew better.

I set myself up as a martyr for a noble cause. I had almost no support from other people in recovery; even my sponsor didn't attend one newcomer meeting. Resentments and blaming for the lack of help began to flow. I had started this noble crusade of one and got annoyed and sad when nobody rallied to my upright endeavor. I persisted and kept the meeting open despite the signs it was a failed exertion. The meeting attendance was low, only three or four people. I prepared specific topics and questions each week. I wanted to impress those attending and rally to my battle cry for sobriety.

Unfortunately, I believe I was alone in my effort; those attending wanted just enough recovery to get their life back in order. But they were not interested in doing any actual work or completing the months of a real honest effort to complete all twelve steps of recovery. Some were mentally unstable and wanted to find something or someone to satisfy themselves and fix them. Not everyone makes it who comes into recovery. The Big Book of Alcoholics Anonymous says, *"Rarely have we seen a person fail who has thoroughly followed our path. Those who do not recover are people who cannot or will not completely give themselves to this simple program, usually men and women who are constitutionally incapable of being honest with themselves."* [5]

I was desperately trying to avenge my sponsee's death, who I connected with so intimately, I failed to heed my lessons from Bob. I was blind to the fact my efforts, while pure in some sense, were a waste. I could assume others in recovery saw and didn't take part because they saw it as a less than noble use. I believe almost to a person. Each addict truly wants permanent recovery for each person who walks into the door. Still, as all people in the recovery rooms can attest, many come, but few stay and experience the blessing of recovery.

Despite the cause, I can see undoubtedly the

---

[5] Bill W., Aaron Cohen, and Bill W., Alcoholics Anonymous: the Original Big Book, 12 Steps, Guides, and Prayers, the Story of How Many Thousands of Men and Women Have Recovered from Alcoholism (Twelve Step Study Guides Publishing, 2015).

effort was misguided and misdirected, and I feel I was the one blind to that effort. As it says in Matthew 7:17-19, *"Likewise, every good tree bears good fruit, but a bad tree bears bad fruit. A good tree cannot bear bad fruit, and a bad tree cannot bear good fruit. Every tree that does not bear good fruit is cut down and thrown into the fire. Thus, by their fruit, you will recognize them" (NIV)*. The tree I had planted was producing nothing, and I was blaming everyone and feeding my ego. I ended the meeting after almost three years of sacrificing time and effort into a failed crusade. While valiant was my effort and noble was my cause, I should have brought the miracle of recovery to my own home. The damage to my marriage would prove irreversible at this point.

    The Hope for Cherokee meeting started with a couple of guys who had the purest of intentions, and the Lord has blessed that meeting. It is flourishing even to this day, with divine endurance. One cannot calculate the lives that have been changed and saved because of that meeting. In my newcomer meeting, I can only account for one failed marriage. I am not saying this as a self-defeating declaration, and I believe the most powerful lessons are negative ones. We are usually the court jester before we are the hero.

    The Lord will bless what he sees as good, and with his blessing comes the fruit. I was blind to that fact for so long because my motives were not the purest. But the essential truth is I may not have changed lives, but I didn't drink. I am still in recovery, and even at my worst, which we will discuss later, I didn't drink alcohol. There may lie the blessing of all my failed attempts to reach people in recovery to stay around long enough so I can be helpful. Like the saying I have heard many times in recovery, "stick around until the miracle happens."

## 5 EMPTY SMILE

My second love has always been pornography; I can also remember my first encounter with pornography, a couple of friends of mine found some dirty magazines in the woods by our house in West Warwick, Rhode Island. I remember those images to this day and can recall them with certainty. It was the early 1980s and way before internet pornography. I knew what I was seeing was wrong; I don't know how, but I knew it was wrong. I just felt guilty for having seen it and embarrassed for liking it. If I didn't feel it was wrong, I wouldn't have hidden it. Those images did more to shape my belief that a woman is supposed to be more than anything else until the last few years. The smile saying, come here, big fellow, was so inviting and alluring. Porn never denied me; it always made me feel wanted. I could take it as I wanted it and when I wanted it. I was in complete control, or so I thought; from that first moment, I would have a love affair with pornography for over thirty years, and with the advent of the internet, which rocketed porn into the fourth dimension.

I can honestly say I never heard of anyone struggling with pornography until I had almost reached rock bottom with it. I don't remember hearing anyone saying that looking at porn was harmful until 2015. I believe pornography is just as addictive as any street drug and even more damaging to the family than any single sin out there. I have always been drawn to pornography since I was exposed to some old dirty magazines we found in the woods, as exhilarating as when I first tasted alcohol. It was an escape; I could immerse myself into the images and create a false reality, if only for a few moments.

My obsession with pornography was always my little secret I never dared to share with anyone because I suspected I enjoyed it more than I should. With extremely low self-esteem, I depended on other's opinions of myself. Porn always gave me the escape into that fantasy where the women instantly attracted me and accepted me as I was; I could create illusions in my head where I was the hero, I was the guy who got the girl every time. It was all the emotional rewards without the mental exertion of real people. The women in the magazines and later the internet were always in the mood and proved more reliable than real people; the benefits of fantasy are short-lived.

Even before I knew the touch of real women, I knew the touch of pornography intimately. I accumulated magazines at an early age of different varieties. I would shuffle between them to keep the excitement level up as I quickly tired of looking at the same images. I would fantasize and arrange in my head with childlike excitement my next pornographic rendezvous when not using them. I was sometimes irritable and discontent before my release. It became one of my only ways of relieving stress. The magazines I accumulated became one of my most prized possessions. As with any addiction, a level of progression that was once exciting and thrilling as time passed would barely get the juices flowing. Management and shuffling of scenarios with different magazines became a stressful occupation. There was much preparation and thought that had to go into each almost daily interlude.

I was almost a daily porn user right from the beginning. As it was with my alcohol use, the honeymoon phase of addictions would slowly ease into addictive behaviors I seemed to skip right over. I was an alcoholic right out of the box, and the same seemed to be true with my porn use. I was an addict right from the beginning, and with my porn and alcohol use in full swing, I would isolate myself for long periods and would only enhance my awkwardly introverted ways. Addiction seemed to grab me quickly. In my naivety, I did not know one could be addicted to pornography. Even in my wildest imagination, I never thought it was even possible. It became my routine and my secret. I told no one; I knew it wasn't healthy. I thought my behavior was always out of step with reality and chose silence and introversion. We never openly discussed masturbation and healthy sexual behavior in my home. I was raised in a Roman Catholic family, and my parents have been married since the early 1960s. Until the advent of smartphones, I don't think anyone thought it was a problem.

I would always make excuses for acting out, claiming boredom, or relieving stress. It was something I would do when I wanted to avoid being alone with myself. Being alone, I could engross myself in a fantasy world. Later, I found out how uncomfortable I became with being alone with myself. We are often the most problematic company to keep. To sit in silence and be with me with nothing else was frightening. With anything you do, the normal becomes mundane quickly, and you become bored. Before online pornography, it wasn't much of a problem using magazines and one's imagination. But that changed quickly as internet access increased.

Ted Bundy was one of America's most publicized and brutal serial killers and rapists, with over thirty murders admitted by himself in the 1970s over seven states. The night before his electric chair execution on January 24, 1989, he was interviewed by Focus on the Family founder Dr. James Dobson. *"In one segment, Bundy told Dr. Dobson about the effect his pornography addiction had on his life. 'Like most other kinds of addiction,' he said, 'I would keep looking for more potent, more explicit, more graphic kinds of material. Like an addiction, you keep craving something which is harder, harder, something which gives you a greater sense of excitement. Until you reach the point that pornography only goes so far.'* Bundy added, *'I've lived in prison a long time now. I've met a lot of men who were motivated to commit violence just like me. And without exception, every one of them was deeply involved in pornography. Without question, without exception, deeply influenced and consumed by addiction to pornography.'"* [6]

    I have heard that it was the only time Ted Bundy had ever told the truth, maybe so or not-- only God knows that. If I am honest with myself, I can relate to the progression of my addiction to pornography. I don't think I have any insight into my capacity until I can admit evil exists in pornography. Only the devil himself can hijack men's minds so well to make him a slave to it hook, line, and sinker. I would be foolish to think I could overcome such an oppressive force in my life without acknowledging the maliciousness that permeated my brain. The realization of good without first recognizing our actions' darkness will prove true goodness to be fleeting.

    I was shocked to find out that marriage doesn't automatically erase sexual lust; I secretly thought marriage was my solution. I assumed I would grow out of it in my active alcoholism. A steady diet of porn caused a great rift between my ex-wife and I that went without discussion for many years. A sober husband who is actively engaging in outreach to help others and is a loving father doesn't seem to be a bad deal. But when the lights go out, and everyone goes to bed, and you know what he is doing and what he is looking at can eat at anyone's soul if given enough time. My cries for sex and demand for openness fell on deaf ears, which drove the wedge between us farther and

---

[6] Luke Gibbons, "Serial Killer Ted Bundy Describes the Dangers of Pornography," CBN News, October 31, 2018, https://www1.cbn.com/cbnnews/us/2018/october/serial-killer-ted-bundy-describes-the-dangers-of-pornography.

farther.

*"Viewers routinely spend hours surfing galleries of porn videos searching for the right video to finish, keeping dopamine elevated for abnormally long periods. But try to envision a hunter-gatherer routinely spending the same number of hours masturbating to the same stick figure on a cave wall. Didn't happen."*— Gary Wilson, Your Brain on Porn: Internet Pornography and the Emerging Science of Addiction.[7]

I had rewired my brain for sex, changed my view of women, and weakened my connection to reality, especially my wife. I knew it was wrong, and I could rationalize and silence my conscience, but never wholly.

Early 2016, the monster in the room had grown so large neither of us could ignore it anymore. I began to admit I had a problem. I attempted to control my porn use to no real avail. I found an ad on a news program website for a church porn addiction recovery group, Conqueror series, done by Ted Roberts.

I found men's groups holding meetings following that series and three in the local area. I confirmed this through the distributor of the series that happily gave me the names of local churches that purchased the group series package. I was excited because a group would be something I was familiar with in Alcoholics Anonymous. I sent my ex-wife the information we discussed, and I must admit I was a little excited. My ex-wife was supportive, as well. I contacted all three local churches the next day who had purchased the series. I left messages at each of the church's phone numbers listed on each of their websites inquiring about a men's group for the conqueror series. After several days and several messages, still no response.

---

[7] Gary Wilson, Your Brain on Porn: Internet Pornography and the Emerging Science of Addiction (Margate, Kent, United Kingdom: Commonwealth Publishing, 2017).

Each day passed with no answer; I became more despondent.

I tested the voicemail of one church I called and left a wrong message on one of the church's voicemails listed in Spartanburg. "Hello, I am Rick Levesque; under the direction of my accountant, I had been advised to reach out to a local charity and make a charitable donation to help with my taxable income. And please call me back as soon as you can." I got a response within two hours. I asked about the group but failed to mention the "charitable donation." They were cordial and church-like but didn't remember anyone buying the series at the church. The company who sold it to them had stated otherwise. I never made a charitable donation.

I was crushed and despondent; I went to rehab with a man who was also a sex addict, and I remember he mentioned going to Sex Addicts Anonymous (SAA). I had already researched this, and there weren't any local meetings. So, I tried one more thing with the church. I attended a men's Sunday School class and felt connected to one man in particular, under discussion with my ex-wife. I decided to see if he would be interested in helping me be accountable in my struggle. I opened up and told him everything; he responded with surprise. I asked him to be my accountability partner; he would pray about it and call me back with a response. I again was hopeful, day after day ticked by until a week later, I called him, and it was then he told me. He prayed on it, and he was sorry he was just too busy and hoped I would understand. I told him I hope I never understand and let an uncomfortable pause materialize.

The irony is that the same man was one of the first men to call me after hearing about my affair; he and a few other men are the reason I am still a Christian today. He saved me when I needed it most. Who disappoints you today very well may be your savior tomorrow. We never know who our Lord uses in our life to guide us. I believe now that these disappointments were simply Jesus pointing me in the direction I should go. That man did the best he could, just like that man I wanted to save me from my alcoholism. The conquering of my demon's responsibility rests on my shoulders alone. I believe the church needs to be more aware and ready to be empathetic of sexual sin. It is nothing new, as the Bible is riddled with sexual immorality; why would today be different? Christians talking about sex can be awkward; it appears taboo even when the subject is simply about what God intended sex to be. So, it's not surprising that for most Christians, the idea of discussing sex addiction is downright frightening. But these struggles need to be addressed; sexual sin is killing our men, and it has destroyed my life and has wreaked havoc on my family. The drug of denial is one I have found to be most alluring and has been the most significant barrier to my relationship with Jesus than anything else. I want to clean up my outside rather than taking the more challenging road and tackling the desires that lead me to sin. As I have heard it said many times in meetings, am I changing, or am I merely polishing a turd. As C.S. Lewis states in Mere Christianity, *"No man knows how bad he is till he has tried very hard to be good. A silly idea is current that good people do not know what temptation means. This is an obvious lie. Only those who try to resist temptation know how strong it is."* [8]

    I have heard it said in countless meetings that we cannot go from "Heal to Halo" in thirty days; I have always become my worst critic. In reflection, the pace of any change in my life has been gradual; in many ways, I am

---

[8] C. S. Lewis, Mere Christianity (Harpercollins Publishers, 2017).

just like George Constanza in Seinfeld, when he would proclaim in a loud shout, "SERENITY NOW." I spent most of my life introducing bad habits into my life; it would be foolhardy to think I could undo that overnight. It says in "1 Corinthians 6:18, *"Flee from sexual immorality. Every other sin a person commits is outside the body, but the sexually immoral person sins against his own body" (NIV)*. I continued to use pornography even after my admission. Still, I began the vicious cycle of trying to hold off looking at it as long as possible, and then when I eventually always succumbed, the cycle of shame began. I would pray for and be dutifully sorry in my heart, and I would feel the love of Christ, and I would feel renewed and go forth boldly. Then days, even weeks, and sometimes months went by with no pornography, and then something would happen internally, and the rationalization would begin in my mind. Once the seed was planted, it only required attention to let it fester.

My eyes wandering was always the first sign; my eyes began straying onto another woman. I had read somewhere not to look upon any women except my ex-wife longer than three seconds. If you looked at a woman for more than three seconds, it served no purpose beyond lust. I have found my eyes always showed how closely I was following God's will rather than my own. It's no surprise when Jesus said in Matthew 6:22, *"The eye is the lamp of the body; so, then if your eye is clear, your whole body will be full of light" (NAV)*. Once I started to gaze upon what wasn't mine, the mind would follow. I would then begin to rationalize my gazing harmless and just mere glances. The justification began to build day by day, moment by moment, until almost inevitably, I would find myself back into the pornography cycle, which almost always was followed by shame and futility.

I remember and can still get completely

despondent, feeling defective. I would tell myself if I was a good man, I wouldn't have to look at the images. I would look at men and their families in public and especially at church and feeling inadequate. I would size them up and know or feel why I couldn't be a truly good man such as them. I would become so angry at myself. Shame and anger consumed me; I would sometimes become irritated and short with my ex-wife and without vocalizing it, which increased the rift between us even more. Pornography robbed me of proper communication with my spouse. I couldn't blame her even a little bit. It would rest the blame of my behavior solely on my feet, which would make me ultimately responsible. I tried to avoid that because I would have to get clean or leave if I accepted full blame. I hadn't been ready to go the extra mile or go to any lengths that desperation would come later.

    I began going to sex-orientated twelve-step groups. The format was very familiar to me, and the literature they read and worked from was the same, but the distance was too far away from my home, yet my ex-wife was still very supportive. With each failure, I became more and more aware that I couldn't do this independently. I became more and more open with my ex-wife about my struggles; she was the only person I truly trusted with my porn addiction. I no longer stayed up late on the computer. I began to change my schedule to make it harder for me to act out. I started working out in the morning, which made me tired in the evening. The unintentional consequence of changing my schedule around to avoid being alone with electronics is that I spent more time with the ex-wife simply because we went to bed together and began to get closer.

    The recovery meetings I was attending for sex addiction comprised a broad spectrum of individuals affected by sexual addictions. It was an eye-opening experience and a completely different world in many ways from the alcohol and drug addiction recovery groups. One cannot talk candidly and openly as one would about other addictions, I believe, simply because of the shame aspect of sexual addictions. In alcohol and drug recovery meetings, the alcohol and drug-fueled exploits were celebrated and often laughed at in the meeting and others in recovery. I found areas where I didn't relate rather than places where I was similar in the meetings. I built some friendships in those meetings but never fully put in the efforts to solidify those relationships because I didn't see myself as one of "those" people.

It's more socially acceptable to be a drunk or former drug addict; I honestly sometimes got a kick out of it once I had several years of recovery under my belt. I was a recovered alcoholic. It almost gave me a sort of speaking street credibility in the church especially. I could always spin a tale or two to make the old ladies in church hair turnabout white. But I would never in a million years process until now that I used to spend hours each night after my kids and ex-wife went to bed with several windows open on my computer looking for the perfect video to masturbate. That I had built up a tolerance and would have to continually look at more and more porn to get the same effect as I did initially. By the grace of God alone was I never caught by my children. I was just as sick as anyone in the meetings, even though my drug of choice was "just" Porn. The behaviors and sickness were there just the same. I just chose not to see the similarities in my addiction to the others because I hadn't gotten that bad, or at least I thought.

Despite my efforts, I still held back some; no addict completely surrenders until they entirely let go of their will. I was still holding back, and this went on for months. I had been around and in recovery for well over a decade- and I knew I hadn't completely surrendered.

Surrender in recovery is to let go completely. I was still trying to control my addiction, and it was managing me; I had finally begun to cease resisting and surrender to His will. That's a lot easier to say than to apply it in one's life. All my schemes to stop looking at porn had failed. I was becoming ready to let go and let God.

I still had full access to the internet on some electronic devices; I remember one Saturday morning. I dumped my guts with my ex-wife and told her everything I was struggling with on the porn. I destroyed a small laptop I had used only to look at porn at night; she knew of the computer's destruction, and I feel it was helpful to build up trust even a little. My smartphone, though, I couldn't destroy that, so I asked her to install a porn blocker on my cell phone and for her to keep the passcode. I was embarrassed, and I was ashamed to ask her, but she was still the one I trusted. I remember feeling so un-masculine and ineffective. It is the same porn blocker I have today. I even held onto a small iPad and used that only in "emergencies" but finally surrendered in October 2018 and destroyed my last electronic device by driving three drill bits through it. That was the last time I looked at pornography but unfortunately was not the last of my struggles with sexual sin, and we will discuss it at length in future chapters.

Years and years of a steady diet of pornography can leave lasting effects for years to come; years later, I have images of pornography pop into my head. The impression it left on me has proved to be the most damaging; it's very naïve to think, as, with any sin, that simple abstinence is the solution. Pornography is the consumption of sexual poison that becomes part of the fabric of the mind. My views on women and intimacy are distorted because of it. Porn was always available. It never denied me; it always did what I wanted. I was in complete control. Porn was never the problem; it was a solution, a terrible solution. For years I used porn as a solution and only made the initial problem worse. I am still trying to understand real intimacy with someone. Porn enables us to piggyback onto someone else's false intimacy and pass it off as our own.

When we download images onto our electronic device or stream them, we may erase every piece of evidence. The image that goes into our brain takes the longest to erase. Also, the mere act of using pornography had transformed me into solitary and unproductive behavior. The secrecy of the entire action degrades healthy communication. Any criticism I would take as an attack on myself. If we create our secret fantasy world where we are always desired and always get the girl, they bend to our will. The after-effects of such private behaviors and ego-driven fantasies consumed for such a long time are felt for years to come.

*"Pornography does not promote sex if one defines sex as a shared act between two partners. It promotes masturbation. It promotes the solitary auto-arousal that precludes intimacy and love. Pornography is about getting yourself off at someone else's expense."* —Chris Hedges, Empire of Illusion: The End of Literacy and the Triumph of Spectacle.[9]

Quitting pornography was but the beginning of my journey. If you were running your engine with no oil, stopping the machine is only the first step. Next, you must assess the damage and take stock of what worked and what has not. Read the manual and then plan to rebuild. In many ways, I didn't do that; I stopped and began to assess my ex-wife and her shortcomings and what she needed to do. The pride and arrogance of quitting conveyed my

---

[9] Chris Hedges, Empire of Illusion: The End of Literacy and the Triumph of Spectacle (New York, USA: Basic Books, 2010).

spouse's criticism and how she didn't measure up to my image of what a woman should be. I had made some steps in the right direction and was still making efforts to change positively. Still, it is effortless to let small accomplishments turn to arrogance with spiritual and mental immaturity. I had conditioned my mind that sex was far more critical than it is, and with a step in the right direction in many senses, I had taken two back. As with my alcoholism, its lingering effects haunted me for years.

Getting honest, cutting off access, and changing the daily habits that facilitated my everyday porn use were the most significant barriers I had to overcome; even today, I follow the same behaviors. I have several people in my life that have struggled with sexual sin, and I can speak with them openly and honestly about sexual sin without judgment and shaming. Finding people to talk about it openly has proved to be the most difficult because of the shame and secrecy of sexual sin. I had been rejected several times, and I believe now that was all part of His plan to guide me where He wanted me to go. I was partly looking for a savior, and when denied even in the slightest, I used it to play the victim card and just give up for a time. The greatest blessing of any addiction is the pain; with enough pain, we become willing; the pain and shame of acting out with pornography become so great I simply don't want to go on living like this.

Changing my daily habits began the process of me starting to feel human again. I started exercising, watching my diet, reading books I always wanted to read, and sleeping an average amount. I began to care for myself. As Aristotle said, "We are what we repeatedly do." I was still looking at porn, but it became infrequent and in spurts. Changing my daily habits did the most to begin the healing process physically. Even today, I try not to stay idle incredibly late
at night and try to get up before the sun is up. If I keep

healthy habits of exercise, proper sleep schedules, and limit my idleness, it keeps the temptation to self-soothe away. I have a lot to learn, but in reflection, and at the height of my porn use, I was not a good Christian family man. But I tried so desperately to portray to the outside world. I had changed my daily habits and shaped other's daily habits.

Cutting off all access to pornography was the one thing I held off until the bitter end. It had become such a part of my life to let it go was incomprehensible. To completely surrender my addiction, my last step to cut was the last remnants of connection. It has been my best friend and my worst enemy all rolled into one. I drove to killing my final link to porn because I knew deep down it has done nothing but caused harm in my marriage and had warped my mind. And I finally become disgusted with myself, enough to go to any lengths to be free.

I started to become honest about my struggles with porn and with others in the rooms of recovery. With the courage to be open about our efforts to others more than I suspected, I found I am not the only one struggling even in the church. I have found that I spent so many years with my secret addiction. Armed with the admission of my powerlessness and surrender. I have learned when and where to disclose this as my years in twelve-step groups; I had learned to be more open than I should be in the wrong way; it has led to some unfortunate encounters, but I would do it again. When we isolate ourselves with our troubles, that's the real sickness because I begin to feel uniquely wretched and worthless; if I do that, I am always in more trouble than necessary. The more I am open and honest with others, the more I found I am not alone in my struggles; not everyone is how they present themselves to the world. I am not cured of my struggle with sexual sin. This would not prove to be the end of my struggles.

## 6 FACEDOWN PHONE

I have been in church most of my life, and I have never felt like I belonged or was worthy of being amongst them. Even as a child sitting in Christ, the King Catholic Church in West Warwick, Rhode Island, I used to look at all the people dressed in their Sunday best. Even at a young age, I felt inferior. I would look at how they interacted as a family and just knew I wouldn't be able to measure up, that somehow, I wouldn't be able to hold those high standards of morality. I knew that I was innately flawed from a very young age and always carried a sense of inferiority. I usually covered this up under many layers of either arrogance or false bravado. Even at the height of my church attendance, I was teaching Sunday school and tithing. I knew those people around me were good people, and I wasn't. They loved their wives, families and were decent men naturally, and it wasn't an act. They naturally got up every morning and did the right thing. I am not naïve enough to think they did everything right, but they did nothing they couldn't fix with superficial repentance and admissions. I understand why people don't go to church. Why face your inferiority, whether it's real or not? It appears natural to the person. I always kept going in one form or the other. I mostly left feeling not refreshed with the spirit but disappointed because I wasn't feeling the same connection with Jesus as everyone else said they felt, so I commonly deduced that I am defective.

I am constantly plagued by my demons ever since I found Christ. I have struggled to do as I should do; I succumb to my inner desires for pleasure to feel just a moment of release and escape from reality, or do I follow Christ. I am a sex porn addict and an alcoholic; I have struggled to refer to myself as only an addict. There are most likely more potential pitfalls my addicted self can fall.

So, in the sense of simplicity, I see myself as just an addict; if it makes me feel good, I will like it, and I will do it until the damaging effects of it permeate my entire life.

Hindsight is always 20/20, I see now as I look at this screen what went wrong, and the funny thing is I knew then. But I covered up the truth to manage the lie.

The Big Book of Alcoholics Anonymous states, *"Each person is like an actor who wants to run the whole show; is forever trying to arrange the lights, the ballet, the scenery, and the rest of the players in his own way. If his arrangements would only stay put, if only people would do as he wished, the show would be great. Everybody, including himself, would be pleased. Life would be wonderful. In trying to make these arrangements, our actor may sometimes be quite virtuous. He may be kind, considerate, patient, generous, even modest, and self-sacrificing. On the other hand, he may be mean, egotistical, selfish, and dishonest. But as with most humans, he is more likely to have varied traits."* [10]

I had created a delusion world where it was okay to step out on my marriage because I occasionally deserved it. It doesn't matter what the reason is that it is self-delusional; it feeds the narcissism needed to betray one's spouse. The delusion that porn was going to protect me from infidelity diminished its usefulness.

Infidelity doesn't start with sex; it begins with sneaky conversations. I know now and knew then the exact point I stepped out of the marriage is when I didn't tell my wife of my temptation. I lacked the courage to do so. I did not have the character to do the right thing; I wanted my cake and ate it. From that moment forward, the internal deception begins; mostly, the most significant

---

[10] Bill W., Aaron Cohen, and Bill W., Alcoholics Anonymous: the Original Big Book, 12 Steps, Guides, and Prayers, the Story of How Many Thousands of Men and Women Have Recovered from Alcoholism (Twelve Step Study Guides Publishing, 2015).

load of bull we shovel is to ourselves. We tell the biggest lie to ourselves because we start to rationalize what we know to be wrong. I believe Paul said it best in Romans 7:15-20, *"I do not understand what I do. For what I want to do, I do not do, but what I hate I do. And if I do what I do not want to do, I agree that the law is good. As it is, it is no longer I myself who do it, but it is sin living in me. For I know that good itself does not dwell in me, that is, in my sinful nature. For I have the desire to do what is good, but I cannot carry it out. For I do not do the good, I want to do, but the evil I do not want to do—this I keep on doing. Now, if I do what I do not want to do, it is no longer I who do it, but it is sin living in me that does it"* (NIV). Once that first lie enters our minds, that behavior we know is wrong, and we immediately begin to cover that lie with a rationalization to make that lie real, at least in our mind. Like the lie is an M&M peanut, the lie is the peanut; we coat the lie with sweet chocolate to sweeten the lie and make it even easier to swallow. Then we rationalize the lie with sweet chocolate. We need to solidify the lie to our new reality, and we add that hard candy shell to protect our lie.

I had started stockpiling mental M&Ms in my mind to a point where I believed I was the victim. Looking at pornography several hours every night while your family was asleep was not a way to satisfy an innately genetic high-sex drive. It was a sickness. But with enough M&Ms in our lives, we can believe anything. My ex-wife would catch me early in our marriage, and eventually, she quit fighting and accepted it as it was. This went on for years and years, and I believed this to be nothing out of the ordinary. Eventually, with M&Ms piling up, infidelity started to become a possibility.

I don't believe anyone wakes up one morning and says they will sin; it starts slowly. In As a Man Thinketh, James Allen states, *"A man is literally what he thinks, his character being the complete sum of all his thoughts."* [11]When we wake up one morning, the seeds of our sins may already have been planted from many days before. James Allen also states, *"A man's mind may be likened to a garden, which may be intelligently cultivated or allowed to run wild; but whether cultivated or neglected, it must, and will, bring forth. If no useful seeds are put into it, then an abundance of useless weed seeds will fall therein and will continue to produce their kind."* It's an inside job.

I believe that the center of all my spiritual growth and my spiritual downfall rests between the six inches between my ears. Porn was watering my garden; it was planting its secret garden. It was growing and growing a little each day. It took years for infidelity to become a possibility, with M&Ms firmly established. And my steady diet of porn was waiting for the right opportunity. We believe ourselves justified to commit sin way before we execute it. With the right amount of rationalization, almost anything is possible.

It's like a gallon of gasoline with the lid off; it's just waiting for the right spark. The first time I stepped out of my marriage, overwhelming guilt followed, but with the buildup of moral degradation and a steady diet of lie-soaked M&Ms, it made our sins' reactions just mere formality be done and lessened with each time. I had checked out of the marriage a long time before; the infidelity was just the inevitable result of years of self-loathing and character growth deprivation. I was officially living not only a mental lie now; it had transformed into a physical one. The feelings of guilt were not enough to go back the second time; the guilt episodes were lessened with each time.

It was cowardice and entitlement, pure and simple. I didn't see it that way when I was doing it. I felt

---

[11] James Allen, As a Man Thinketh (New York: St. Martin's Essentials, 2021).

like I deserved it. After all, if she only acted a certain way, I wouldn't be compelled to do this. I was the victim. It's very easy when one is in that whirlwind of self-delusion to point all the blame on her shoulders; she wasn't a perfect wife by any stretch of the imagination; she was flawed just as I was. No matter how imperfect she was, I was the one who quit on us and had an affair. The giant bucket of manure that is shoveled is the one we scoop to ourselves. As Fyodor Dostoevsky in The Brothers Karamazov says, *"Above all, don't lie to yourself. The man who lies to himself and listens to his own lie comes to a point that he cannot distinguish the truth within him or around him, and so loses all respect for himself and for others. And having no respect, he ceases to love."* [12]

Once the affair transitioned to a physical form, everything changed, and the lies began piling up, the secret life began. I would be lying to say it was not exhilarating and self-shaming all at the same time. If infidelity were dull, nobody would be doing it. I am not blaming anyone or anything for my unfaithfulness. I had isolated myself from my family; the years of pornography were in one sense as damaging as I never left the realm of fantasy. The frequency of this happening in our society should never dull the magnitude of infidelity. In many ways, it is the equivalent of murder performed in a video game versus reality; the leap is that severe.

Fantasies and pornography, while damaging and extremely detrimental in my life, as I have discussed, can fade and heal far more effectively than physical actions. You cannot undo, forget, or fade away in your memory once it goes to physical unfaithfulness. There is no greater betrayal, and it can never be undone. Once that level of betrayal is done, every victim has no alternative but to

---

[12] Fyodor Dostoevsky, *Brothers Karamazov* (S.L.: Picador, 2021).

examine how you perceive that person thoroughly. Everyone I know was forced to see me differently; I was no longer who I was, infidelity has rocked the very fabric of my identity.

With my years of sponsoring men in recovery, I had, in many ways, the foundation of a secret life already laid down. The anonymity of twelve-step recovery meant that my family was already conditioned to me keeping others' anonymity. The anonymity of recovery protects those looking for help. I would get phone calls from men in recovery that I was working within the program and would have to step outside to talk to them. The cornerstone of recovery is not advertising to anyone who exactly is in recovery. Anyone who struggles with drugs or alcohol, admitting you have a problem and actively seeking help is a severe cause of concern. Most of the concerns are unfounded and strictly pride-based, but I know persons with susceptible jobs or family predicaments that anonymity was something they relied upon. I have heard it said at many meetings, "be free to share what you heard here but not who you saw here."

Under this umbrella of anonymity rested the track that enabled me to facilitate my infidelity. With years of spending so much time trying to help other men in recovery, the mere transition to texting and spending time with a member of the opposite sex raised no suspicion. I had built up my credibility over ten years in recovery, sponsoring people. Even in the throes of my alcoholism, no rational person would ever step out of his marriage physically. I did place myself in some compromising situations. I even tried to kiss our neighbor once after my ex-wife and I were first married, which made being neighborly challenging. The shame and embarrassment that I brought to my ex-wife must have been crushing for a newlywed. Messing with women was always a sure-fire way to kill your buzz, and I never seemed to have the energy to do both. Towards the end of my drinking, my equipment wasn't functioning correctly because of heavy alcoholism for so long, doubtful it would have been physically possible.

I have told things to myself and my ex-wife, and I believed them to be accurate when I said it to them. I don't think I lied, but now I think it wasn't true. We begin to see a more authentic, more honest reality with honest reflection and time, so earlier insights cannot be dismissed as un-false but simply as altered to our newest perspectives. I only bring up this because what truth we feed ourselves today isn't and shouldn't be the truth we provide ourselves in the future. A careful and prayerful examination can reveal many things, and writing this book has forced me to reflect honestly on what happened and what I can do to prevent it in the future. I may very well be the most critical person, which helps in writing this book.

I can look back with certainty at my actions and patterns that enabled this deceit to go on. My cell phone was deemed off-limits to anyone besides myself; it was never discussed or was that rule ever laid down. It just metastasized from the anonymity of recovery. Men I worked with would have problems with spouses, jobs, kids, and just life in general. The thinking was I made myself available 24/7, so if they needed someone, they would talk to me rather than reach for a drink or a drug. The texts and calls were always at the most inconvenient times. It was perfectly natural for me to leave the house to text or call someone. After all, there was a revolving door of men in recovery I was helping. They never seemed to stay long enough to keep names and problems straight.

If my phone was not on my person, it was always laid face down, so when I got a text or call, anyone passing by my phone couldn't see what was sent and from who. I can see that now as the one behavior that enabled me to transition from nobly spreading the message of experience, strength, and hope of recovery to having an affair. That one behavior of keeping my phone down enabled the infidelity to transition from anonymity to secrecy and betrayal. This behavior of laying the phone down in the house started with the best intentions, but I used it for the worst of them.-

If one thought of how my ex-wife could be so easily deceived, one would be foolhardy to pass judgment too quickly on that. Do not fool yourself into a false sense of security that you are above being fooled so quickly, considering easily laid out facts and armed with honest admissions or wrongs done. It's easy to solve the riddle if you already have the answer to the puzzle. I had an easy ten years of sponsoring men in recovery and post-discovery discussions with her. She had her suspicions. If you are reading this book and questioning if your spouse is cheating on you, he or she probably is. It may look, walk, and talk like a duck, but that doesn't always prove entirely accurate.

I nearly robbed my entire family of their past, present, and future in an instant. The man they lived with and thought I was turned out to be a lie. All the memories they had with me were robbed and had to be reevaluated. Each memory had to be reassessed to what they thought was a pleasant memory and cross-checked with the dates of my affair, vacations, birthdays, holidays, and intimate moments. Even the fondest of memories will most likely have to be discarded when I was with her. If they fall into that category, they must be recategorized when my affair was going on, no matter what it is. The personal impact will have to be dumped like garbage. I did my best to recall the dates, and it went off and on for almost two years. That's a lot of memories that everyone must dump.

The man everyone knew was nothing but a mirage, a mere image of what he appeared to be. People are hurt most of all by deception; they can't handle betrayal. Having the rug pulled out from underneath themselves, especially by those they love and respect, does them in. To love someone is to be vulnerable and have someone so close take part in deception that magnitude is earth-shattering. One can only think if I truly can love while knowingly and intentionally engaging in such trickery and for as long as I did.

*"You're saddled with a partner who has checked out of the marriage. Why? Because of entitlement, cowardice, and crap life skills. Why? Because that is their character — when the going gets less than optimal, they cast about."*—Tracy Schorn, Leave a Cheater, Gain a Life: The Chump Lady's Survival Guide. [13]

I took the coward's way; instead of fighting for my marriage when I was in it, I succumbed to temptation. I have had countless people tell me I should fight for my marriage after D-day. Most times that feels good to say, and it is empowering, but it is like fighting after the battle is already decided

I could very well claim it was my addiction or addictive mind that drove me to infidelity, but we both know that is an excuse. One who would blame any addiction on any forethought behavior would be someone who doesn't want to take responsibility for actions but force others around them to change to suit their addiction. I lacked the moral character to fight for my marriage when it was most important when I was in it. As I write this, I am days away from my official divorce hearing, and I have nothing to gain or lose by my honesty and open admission. I have failed to include the details of my infidelity, which is

---

[13] Tracy Schorn, *Leave a Cheater, Gain a Life: the Chump Lady's Survival Guide* (Perseus Books Group, 2016).

not by accident because it simply doesn't matter.

    I believe I am more prone to addictive behavior and thus have to be more vigilant, just like some soil is more apt to grow fruit than vegetables. In a steady diet, the thing about pornography is that it is a fertilizer that almost inevitably corrupts even the most fertile mind. I don't believe that there is more of a sinister mind and soul warping device than internet pornography. If you wanted to corrupt an addictive-prone individual, give him free, easily accessible images and videos of sex on the internet. And the kicker, make the church silent on the matter, and it festers my sense of entitlement that is irrelevant post infidelity. It's not like I was unaware I had addictive tendencies; I had been sitting in recovery meetings for well over a decade.

    I deceived everyone for my pleasure for an extended period because I never thought I'd get caught. I believe that infidelity has little to do with sex; and more to do with deception and sin than anything else. Little lies are used to cover up big lies. When it began, when it ended, how often it happened are ways to minimize the impact. If you stab someone to death, it doesn't matter if you stabbed him six times or a hundred, with a spoon or butcher knife; the result is the same.

# 7 D-DAY FEBRUARY 12, 2020

On February 12, 2020, around 6 p.m., I received a phone call on my cell from an unidentified number; I had given my number to some new recovery members, so it wasn't unusual. On the phone was the woman I had an affair with off and on for almost two years. She had found out about a non-sexual encounter with another woman in recovery and texts from that other woman. She was irate and was coming to my home to tell my ex-wife everything; I pleaded with her not to because my son was home. She was unfazed. I kept calling and pleading with her, but she was incensed. I met her in the driveway and said nothing. Her appearance was disheveled, and she had a white film around her mouth from something. She was noticeably high or drunk. I did not block her as she forcefully barged into my home in a fit of rage. She found my ex-wife in the kitchen. I was in shock, but I knew this was my creation, and it was time to pay the piper.

In the most uncomforting and wrathful manner, she yelled in my ex-wife's face that she had an affair with me (of course, those aren't the words she used, and her language was curse-laden and too vulgar to repeat, and my son heard the initial outburst). As my companion of twenty years was getting her soul ripped out, the sheer volume of her voice, I only thought of my son.

I grabbed my son, went upstairs with him, and tried to console and reassure him as best I could. My son was locked on me visually with a focus I have never seen before. He had so many questions about why that woman was in his home. Why she was yelling at his mother, and why his mother was so upset. I had no answers to many of the questions. I didn't know how to communicate what was going on effectively. I was in shock and knew I was leaving the house shortly and expressing my love and bond to him. I only knew my secret was out, and those I called my family, who just a few moments ago thought and believed I was a good Christian man, but saw the truth I had been hiding in a very disgusting, violent manner. I wouldn't have wished this encounter on my worst enemy. The intent was to hurt and inflict tremendous pain on my ex-wife, and it did. To this day, I still do not know entirely what was said; I could only hear brief periods of violent outbursts.

My ex-wife heard enough and kicked the woman out; after a brief pause, I faced her as I knew what was coming. The moment I had been dreading for the longest of times, she looked at me with a tear-soaked face. In her face, I could see the emotional beating she had just taken and asked if it was true; I said yes. I never fought it at all. I knew in the pit of my heart fighting was only going to make it worse. I had surrendered and knew my sins have come to the surface. I can just try to grasp the magnitude of hurt that was being thrust upon her in the most insensitive of ways. The affair was presented in the most hurtful ways and was done maliciously and with the intent of revealing a secret while inflicting maximum pain. I knew my ex-wife for most of my adult life and have never seen such hurt on someone's face as I had seen on hers; she was shattered. I can close my eyes now and visualize her face to the smallest detail; it is a face of disgust and pain. She told me to get out. I just nodded in agreement and began collecting my things. She began making phone calls to her family, notifying them of what had transpired. With each phone call, my reputation was dragged into the mud where it rightly belonged. I was an adulterer, liar, narcissist, and had fooled everyone I know into believing I was someone I wasn't. I deserved fully every embarrassment and shame that was happening, and that was coming. I cannot even pretend to understand the weight that must have been thrust upon my ex-wife's shoulders at that moment. As a mother, she wasn't only trying to comprehend the hurt upon herself but also the damage for her two children.

My son went frantic, not fully grasping what had gone on and what is going to happen next. He was asking questions like, who is going to be my dad? Are you coming back? Will I ever see you again? My efforts to console him seemed futile. As I left, he was confused and frantic despite my best efforts to comfort him. I looked him straight in the face and told him how much I loved him and that I would always be his dad. I also told him I would see him real soon, but I had a job for him. The job was to care for his mother and sister and hug them often. As I drove away, I saw his broken frame in the driveway locked on me. I had just witnessed the breaking of two out of the three most influential people in my life. My family's whole life, as they knew, was crushed in an instant. The one person they came to rely on turned out to be someone so different. I can only imagine it is as if they never knew me.

My daughter was at church youth that night; she called me frantic as I was driving. She knew something was terribly wrong, but not exactly sure what. I have no idea if she tried calling her mother, but she called me. She wanted to know what was going on. I was entirely trying to grasp the gravity of what was going on myself. The young lady I was talking to was the same one who looked at me with pride and admiration. I had told her the woman I had an affair with had come to the house. I said what had happened; she began wailing and asked why and then hung up the phone. That was the last I heard her voice for several months, and it has destroyed our relationship; I fear forever. My daughter was always daddy's little girl; we always shared a special bond stemming from my early recovery from alcoholism, and that bond I fear was broken that night. It broke my heart to tell her so that I can only imagine the pain to hear it. I can only attempt to understand what pain I had caused her by telling the father she thought she knew never was.

I recently got a new sponsor, one I felt could be completely honest about my issues. We were still in the honeymoon phase of our relationship, getting to know each other. I had asked him to sponsor me in recovery, and I remember explicitly being impressed with his honesty and openness of his fallibility. He was getting a tattoo removed from his neck; I had assumed it was because it was a neck tattoo. The night I asked him, he shared openly that the tattoo on his neck he was getting removed was his sister's name. He was just as puzzled as anyone else would be since he didn't particularly care for his sister that much. But he continued to confess that drugs and alcohol had warped his judgment and caused him to make rash, dumb decisions. He also noted that he kept the tattoo to remind him of his poor choices but was getting it removed because he felt that phase of his life was over. I was amazed by his frankness and honesty in front of others. I longed to be that transparent and felt confident working with him in my recovery on all levels.

As per standard protocol in recovery rooms, in times of crisis, you call your sponsor. I immediately called my sponsor as I left my house and told him what had happened and that I would sleep in my office. He was shocked as we were still getting to know each other, and it had been quite a considerable length of time since my infidelity; it was surprising for it to come out now after so much time had passed. He informed me he was going to meet me at a coffee shop in Shelby. I was emotionally drained and just wanted to get somewhere and unfold mentally what had happened. We argued back and forth on meeting or not. I was trying to talk him out of it and reassure him I was fine; he was insistent. The shock of the night hadn't hit me yet. He wouldn't take no for an answer; in his words, he just wanted to look at me and make sure I was going to be alright. I can't help but feel that I wished I had the courage and conviction to be so bold when others needed me.

I finally agreed to meet him in downtown Shelby for a few moments; I believe I saved my life by talking to him. I had what we call in the rooms of recovery a moment of clarity. I was just ardently drained and in a lot of emotional pain. I could not see my life ever getting past this night. I believed my life was over, and it never could get better; it was going to continue forever hurting like that. You try to cheer yourself up, but it's useless. You cannot look past the pain. It was all self-imposed pain. I cannot even grasp the complexity of my ex-wife and kids' pain at that very moment. I had talked myself into a dark area of my mind where we don't let God or any other good in. Convinced that if I dared to do it tonight, it would be just a bad night for my family, and in doing the honorable thing by shooting myself, I could die with a semblance of honor and avoid any further embarrassment to them. My family could move on with the insurance I had, and they would be taken care of, and they could move on respectfully with a truly good man in my place. Despite my thinking in a moment of sanity that night, I did what I didn't want to do.

I asked him to hold on to my gun that I kept in my glove box. He took it willingly despite him being a felon and not legally allowed to possess a firearm. He took the chances of negative consequences for himself without hesitation. Because I can suspect he knew I did not need it around considering what just happened. I admire his courage; looking back, it was probably regarded as foolhardy on his part but showed the strongest one of the most notable acts of love I have ever seen. He knew the consequences and what would happen to him if he was caught with that gun but took it willingly and without hesitation. What comes to mind is John 15:13, "Greater love has no one than this: to lay down one's life for one's friends" (NIV). He was willing to risk everything he had worked for since he left prison to help his fellow man.

As I lay awake in my office under the desk that night, it hit me with a tidal wave of emotion. I believe this to be true; if my sponsor hadn't taken my gun, I would have shot myself with almost certainty that night. It hit me with a fury, and I could not see my way out of the pain. I wanted the pain to stop, and I felt it was the best thing I could have done for my family. I wanted to spare them the shame that I knew was coming. My addiction and deceit had stripped me of everything I loved and valued. I was the sole creator of the misery I had felt and was trying to understand what pain I had caused those around me. I had failed to understand and deal with the evil within myself. When that emerges, it is never at the most convenient time.

A dear friend of mine said many times in recovery meetings, "When you are alone in your head, you are bad neighborhood talking to a fool." In the decade since I first heard this, I have never found it to be untrue. After D-day, I lived with my parents for about a week. I spent the first weekend in their spare room staring out the window, replaying the events in my head. My parents did their best to console me and make me comfortable, and despite my self-imposed isolation in their spare room, I appreciated the company. I do not feel it was safe for me to be alone. I began to grasp what exactly happened, and the blame for it all rests entirely on my shoulders. It was bound to happen;

the years of looking at pornography and the affair had warped my mind so much; I don't think I could ever have truly grasped the concept of intimacy with my ex-wife. I had a dysfunctional view of sex. The night of my life crumbling apart was my opportunity to reset my sex life. I spent hours just staring. I couldn't eat, sleep, or even speak more than a sentence or two without bursting into tears. Each day seemed to get worse. I was on the fence spiritually; I didn't want to pray. I just sat and stared and stayed in my head; this pain I felt resulted from my false entitlement and lack of character. I was reaping what I had sewn and deserved every bite.

What about my wife of twenty years? Until the woman came to our home, my ex-wife believed she was married to a good godly man. She thought our problems were in the past. That belief was snatched away from her in an instant by an inebriated scorned ex-lover. The history she knew turned out to be false; her future just vanished. Her best friend turned out to be a lie to her for almost two years and sneaking behind her back to share the most intimate part of a marriage with a known drug abuser. I cannot even begin to understand the emotions she was feeling. Having your heart ripped out of your chest like that is a pain I wouldn't wish on my worst enemy. The secrets we keep have a funny way of clawing their way to the surface once they rear their ugly head, no telling what the fallout out from it will be.

I have heard it often said that children are resilient and can bounce back; I do not believe it. I think their immaturity masks their inability to comprehend what is happening entirely and can never effectively communicate what happened. They are forever changed. Everyone's entire future, past and present, was ripped from them; what they thought and believed turned out to be false. I sometimes feel that children being resistant to divorce is a way to shrug off their impact. My experience is that it is real, and they are not resilient. They may be silent because they do not know the words to use, but neither less pain is there, and it is real. In the following weeks, I spent more and more time with my son, and even the first time, if I paid attention, I knew he was forever different. He was excited to see me because he loved his dad, but if I mentioned anything to do with the divorce, I could instantly sense his tenseness.

My children have been raised their entire life, with the center of their life being the core commitment of my ex-wife and me that we were one in all things. In an instant, their reality was shattered; their whole conception of what commitment is was destroyed in a flash. Their mom and dad's image of being together exclusively has been drastically altered to where I seemed to be a stranger. I went from hero to zero in an instant. My identity in both my children's eyes was changed from one of integrity to one based on lies. I became an instant stranger to everyone and not trusted; I must have been viewed so differently. Once we see someone in a new light, we can never go back to the light we once basked in for others to see. A truth, once revealed, can never be unrevealed.

My family is shattered. I hope I have the strength to rebuild it; I want to make this suffering worthwhile. There is simply no way for me to grow and overcome this unless I learn to put others above myself in all things. I am not naive to the fact that my sin and my selfishness had misshapen my core family unit into something I wished it hadn't. Like molding silly putty, we cannot manipulate the putty enough to back where it was; the more we do so, the worse we distort it. My family cannot ever go back to the way it was before D-day. My family will never look at me the same. It has changed because what they know now versus then.

As Ana Nogales says in Parents Who Cheat: How

Children and Adults Are Affected When Their Parents Are Unfaithful, *"When children of any age learn of a parent's infidelity, they usually find it extremely difficult—if not impossible—to trust that someone they love will not lie to them, reject or abandon them, or otherwise cause them pain somewhere down the road. They often learn not to put their faith in love, and they may also learn that they are not worthy of receiving monogamous love, because according to the evidence, their betrayed parent clearly wasn't."* [14] They had nothing to do
with my bad decisions, but how could they not feel that they were not worthy? Nothing could be further from the truth. I loved my family but failed to honestly express that love correctly because of my narcissism and false self of entitlement, and cowardice. I stepped out on my marriage and never gave the slightest thought of what my actions would do to others I supposedly loved.

    I was simply a mirage; how much I must have crushed my children's perception of trust. My ex-wife trusted me with the most sacred of all things anyone could be trusted with, her future. She had long forgone any plans for her fate to be solely with me alone. She had no plan B, and we both had, as it says in Genesis 2:24, *"For this reason, a man shall leave his father and his mother and be joined to his wife; and they shall become one flesh" (NAS)*. She did not know it, but I had secretly split myself from her in my infidelity, and once my sin was revealed, she was left holding all the skin she had put into the game. I secretly changed the rules without her knowledge. Disloyalty to my ex-wife and our family unit's very core has rocked the bedrock of the family unit's foundation. I was defective and not worthy of them; I believed I was entitled to more in my mirage state,

---

[14] Ana Nogales and Laura Golden Bellotti, Parents Who Cheat: How Children and Adults Are Affected When Their Parents Are Unfaithful (Deerfield Beach, FL: Health Communications, 2009).

but they were worth more than I was willing to give. As Tracy Schorn talks about in Leave a Cheater, Gain a Life: The Chump Lady's Survival Guide, I was a sparkly turd shiny on the outside but inside still just a turd. [15]

I am not trying to sound simple or to make excuses. With my steady diet of pornography, narcissism, and blame-shifting, I didn't believe the impact of my infidelity would be this great after so much time. It has conclusively convinced me of the utter destructiveness of my behavior. I yanked the warm blanket of security in the core family unit and pulled it from under all of them. They catapulted into a
state of emotional free fall, with no end in sight. I am trying to understand the hell I put them through, but I can't. I cannot see their world no matter how much I try, not as it is but only through the lenses of who I am. Apologies and regrets are almost useless words that do nothing more than reinforcing the futility of changing the past. As Stephen Covey says in The 7 Habits of Highly Effective People: Powerful Lessons in Personal Change, *"You can't talk your way out of problems you behave yourself into."* [16]

D-day will continue to be one of the most impactful days of my life. Talk is cheap; our morality is existential. What we do outside is what we believe on the inside. Our words are almost meaningless. As I write, my daughter will not speak to me; the impact of D-day has proven too much for my little girl, who I cherish. I am doing my best to convey to anyone what my sin has brought upon my family. I cannot change the past or erase D-day, but I must believe that what matters most right

---

[15] Tracy Schorn, Leave a Cheater, Gain a Life: the Chump Lady's Survival Guide (Perseus Books Group, 2016).

[16] Stephen R. Covey, The 7 Habits of Highly Effective People (London: Simon & Schuster UK Ltd., 2020).

now is how I respond to D-day.

I believe now infidelity is a family sin; it isn't just a sin against your wife. D-day destroyed my family. I do not know why that woman did what she did, especially in how she revealed it. It was done with one purpose: to cause the maximum amount of pain. I remember pleading with her before she barged in, not to dissuade her from confession but to do it another time. Her actions that day and since have proved malicious and unbalanced. This is irrelevant as my actions before D-day had placed her at my doorstep that night and nobody else's. We never truly get away with anything; there are always repercussions for the choices we make today.

Winston Churchill's words declaring the actual D-day as a day that will live in infamy come to mind, and I know every day since February 12, 2020, has been affected by that day. It has changed the entire trajectory of my life. Many days, especially right after D-day, were the worst of my life. I spent many days staring at a Glock pistol wanting to swallow it, and I would tell myself I will kill myself tomorrow and kept postponing it. One of my worst days was a Sunday, about a month after D-day; I spent the entire day staring at my cell phone. I had gotten ready, dressed, and cleaned up. I was convinced my daughter would call me that day so we could talk; she never did and hadn't since. It was my absolute lowest, I believe, or close to it.

I have heard people say that their dad or mom were their heroes. My daughter has always been mine. I am convinced she saved me from the pits of my alcoholism. She loved me when I was unlovable and when nobody else trusted me enough to love me. She has always been my angel. I can still feel her little hand in mine as we walked together on our latest adventure. I vividly remember camping. She caught me crying after I thought she had gone to sleep. I was crying because I was sober for a little while, yet I felt crushed by the weight of my new life sober. She wrapped her tiny arms around me, kissed my tear-filled cheek, and told me everything was going to be alright. I believe now, as I did then, she was an angel sent by Jesus to save me from myself. And almost a decade and a half later, I broke that same little girl's heart again. My deception and shattering of her family have proved to be the most challenging truth to swallow.

    I see the same cycle continue as post-D-day. I had my son every weekend, and he has proven to be my second angel. We have continued to grow beyond measure in our relationship. Several times he had to wrap his arms around his father and hug him. I look forward to each weekend with much anticipation because I know he loves me, and I love him. His attention and companionship have proved to be the only spark in the vortex I have created. Without him in my life, I may have succumbed to my shame and guilt. Several people I knew from my old church and people in recovery looked beyond my sin and saved me. The following Monday, four men called me, and I cannot put into words what their phone calls meant to me.

    I cannot grasp and put into words my feelings of remorse for my sin towards my family. When I look at my son and catch glimpses of my daughter at her home, I pray I can change so they can be proud of their dad. My children are my heroes because they both saved me when I needed saving. They loved me when I didn't deserve it, just like Jesus has.

# 8 MODERN-DAY LEPROSY

I believe without a doubt; things happen for a reason. And something that could be the worst thing that has happened to you turns out to be the best thing. A good majority of people I end up breaking my anonymity about my alcoholism respond differently. Congratulations, you must be so proud, or a simple "I am sorry." I have always understood the first response as people don't understand the recovery of grace. My usual answer is, "I did nothing; it was all God." I know people responding in a way unorthodox to something they do not understand. Getting clean to most persons is the equivalent of losing twenty-five pounds. They say if you try hard enough, you can do it, and this isn't entirely untrue. It requires effort and constant vigilance to be successful, but most of all, it is grace.

I heard early in recovery that only one in ten make it their first year of recovery. I was blown away after hearing that but soon discovered it was a fact. And it gets worse as the years progress. Few are ready for the complete honesty and commitment required, or to say it better; few are desperate enough. For years, I was in recovery meetings where I arrived late, told them lies, went drunk, and once deceitfully accepted my two-month clean chip drunk. I believe I even cried a little when they let me speak and they just told me about the ever-familiar mantra "keep coming back." It was not exactly a high point of my recovery career, but they listened intently and didn't interrupt me. I have seen similar spectacles that others have done in recovery. But I must tell myself as I have heard it said in meetings many times, "But for the Grace of God there go I."

As I have learned, grace is getting something for nothing but must be with true repentance, in the most basic theological terms. Grace is love, a gift. I have heard many a preacher preach at length and go on and on and on about grace. I was just as confused about grace at the end of their sermon as in the beginning. As has been the case in most of my life, the simple answers resonate the most loudly with me. The simple wisdom I had heard in the rooms of recovery absent of theological whims has proved to be the most useful in my spiritual walk. This essential spirituality has sustained me and has begun the journey that I still understand God's will. I have heard it said that many would go down as alcoholic martyrs in the recovery rooms, so we must take this God stuff seriously.

One day you talk to someone in a meeting, and their life is going great. And then, at the next meeting, there are not there; they had "gone back out." If you are lucky, you may find what happened to them, and they may make it back. I often remember talking to someone who lifted you when you were down, gave you words of encouragement, and then I would go to a gas station and see that same person all ruffled in a mug shot photo of a local paper. Moments like that were always sad, but I began to understand what grace was. I was and am now nothing special. But I am a child of God like anyone else. I was blessed or cursed with the same addiction as them. Why was I the one reading about them in the paper and not the other way around? It's a question I have asked myself over and over, with no plausible answer except for one word. Grace.

During my time in recovery, the revolving doors of recovery continued. Many come for help, some stay a while, and but few stay for long. I knew deep down I was no better or worse than anyone else. I believed my time would come when I would succumb to my addiction and be back off at the races once more. And once again, I would be writing more of my story. Providentially that day has not come yet; I always blush and feel bad when people congratulate me on my recovery time when they find out. I know I don't deserve any recognition; I met better-suited people in recovery that didn't make it; why am I here clean and sober and not them? I have no explanation but one word: grace. With my addiction to pornography and me, especially with the revelation of my infidelity, I found an increasingly small community I could talk to openly open such things. I had tried to reach out once to one of the deacons at our church in 2011; I told him just in general terms I was having a problem with porn and asked if he knew of any resources to help me. He listened intently and said he would "pray" about it. The following week he stopped me in the hallway at our church and went and got the preacher and told the preacher, "Here is the guy I told you about." We huddled up and prayed together like one would at a football game.

No more was ever said about it; prayer is an integral part of my recovery, but it isn't a magic elixir to be used once, and "oh that's better" glad Jesus saved me from that... I trusted that man with my confidence, and he betrayed it and told the preacher cloaked in good-hearted Christian hood. It was almost five years before I reached out for help again. Incidents like that have fueled my passion for writing this book. In recovery, anonymity and strict confidence are honored as a virtue above most. I am not saying I have never seen anonymity broken; in recovery, it happens. It is tragic, and it destroys lives, but in the rooms of recovery, the breaking of anonymity is the extreme exception, and I have only seen it personally just twice.

People go into recovery armed with the full knowledge they are losers and or sinners right from the onset and can only go up from there. There is a lot of truth saying that those in recovery didn't get there because they acted up in Sunday school. They come to recovery because their life is not working for them and they had nowhere else to go. Why should the sinners go to recovery and the saints go to church? Mark 2:16-17 says, *"When the teachers of the law who were Pharisees saw him eating with the sinners and tax collectors, they asked his disciples: 'Why does he eat with tax collectors and sinners?' On hearing this, Jesus said to them, 'It is not the healthy who need a doctor, but the sick. I have not come to call the righteous but sinners" (NIV).*

When my infidelity was revealed, people I prayed with and taught in Sunday school wouldn't acknowledge my presence among them. It hurts any way you slice it. I hate to report it happened more than I would like to admit, and it shocked from whom it happened. When your life is in turmoil, you find out who your friends are; even family members who you have looked after and cared for will turn their back on you. None of that matters; people are people, we are flawed, and it's not for me to condemn and pass judgment on anyone. If you have read the previous chapters, you are probably convinced or can see by now; I have no halo on my head. So, who am I to convict anyone? As Brennan Manning says in The Ragamuffin Gospel, *"To live by grace means to acknowledge my whole life story, the light side, and the dark. In admitting my shadow side, I learn who I am and what God's grace means."* [17] I have a light and dark side to myself; if I point out my experience with the dark side, I must also point out the light. I must never fool myself into believing I and others are as good as we present ourselves. Our beloved savior sent a message to the sinner covered in shame and to the local church that the church is often ritualistic and slow to forgive for fear of appearing lax and liberal. The number of people who

---

[17] Brennan Manning, The Ragamuffin Gospel (Colorado Springs, CO: Multnomah Books, 2015).

have fled the church because it was too patient and too compassionate is insignificant. Still, the number who have fled due to forgiveness and ostracism is tragic. First Corinthians 13:4-5 states, *"Love is patient, love is kind. It does not envy, it does not boast; it is not proud. It does not dishonor others, it is not self-seeking, it is not easily angered, it keeps no record of wrongs" (NIV)*.

Many Christians do not know how to approach those that have fallen into sin. They do not have any experience with that sin. Many have never failed to where many of us have struggled with sin. They are at a loss for words and do not know or have experience reaching out to others. It may come across as judgment or indifference when it merely may not be known how to formulate the correct words to reach out. I can't say the right words to communicate the love of someone who has lost a limb. I am flawed just as much, and if not more than anyone. I hope this book will help Christians to reach out even if they do not feel comfortable, as we are all worth love. The first real human was a murderer (Cain), and it has been going downhill ever since. My five-year-old daughter knew to hug me when she caught me crying outside my tent. She was young and didn't fully understand why I was crying, but she knew I needed love.

Any organization is tainted right from the beginning because of one thing, "people." We are all flawed. It is easy for me to take this incident and stew on it, and use it as an excuse to put the entire church into a box. Even Jesus said in Matthew 7:3-5, *"Why do you see the speck that is in your brother's eye, but do not notice the log that is in your own eye? Or how can you say to your brother, 'Let me take the speck out of your eye,' when there is the log in your own eye? You hypocrite, first take the log out of your own eye, and then you will see clearly to take the speck out of your brother's eye" (ESV)*.

The casual reference that we are all sinners that I have heard in the church simply isn't enough when I am not actively engaging in major sin and not tempted by anything. This does not prevent me from sinning. I am an admitted drunkard, porn addict, and adulterer; if you are reading this and do not think that if you were in my exact shoes, you would fare better than me. That you would be able to live a Godly Christian life and resist temptation where I had failed, I empathize with your arrogance. One cannot be so arrogant to assume their holiness in all situations. I am not that powerful, and I have a suspicion you aren't either. There is only one I know of who could resist the devil in the desert, and I am sure you aren't Him.

There is a culture of service and loyalty that I believe the church could learn a lot from twelve-step groups. I have had the pleasure to be in both worlds. Each world believes they are superior to the other. I have heard quite a few preachers say that you don't need recovery; you only need Jesus in your life. In recovery meetings, I often hear church people are a bunch of phonies and liars. Countless times I have called many churches, and they don't answer their phone or return voice mails. Yet, you call just about anyone in recovery, and they almost without hesitation call you back and meet you anywhere at any time. I have also seen church members give vast amounts of money with no hope of recognition. One side shouts hypocrites, and the other accuses them of false discipleship.

I have heard quite a few preachers tell me that "You don't need AA (Alcoholics Anonymous) or NA (Narcotics Anonymous) or any twelve steps. All you need is Jesus." Are they wrong? Well, not entirely. Years ago, there was a local preacher who came to meetings at my homegroup. He would sit in the back, and if questioned, he always said he was researching someone in "his congregation." I handed my phone number to him and invited him to coffee, but he never called. All us drunks saw through his mirage. He came to about a dozen meetings, and I heard nothing more until a couple of months later. In the local paper, I read that he had gotten a DUI charge and was voted out of his church.

Nate Larkin of the Samson Society says, *"Let's face it: the reason many guys have stopped telling the truth in church is because most churches actively discourage truthfulness. Even in Christian men's groups, the cost of candor is usually painfully high, the punitive response to it swift and decisive."*[18] If you are reading this and are a Christian church member or Bible study and having real problems that were secret, could you talk openly about it to that group with no fear of retribution? Would it initiate others to speak openly and honestly, seriously? Even if you have no real problems, what if you heard someone tell of some things? What would you do, really do, no church fluff, what you would do? Would you hug them and pray with them, or would you try to help them? If you didn't know the answers, would you find someone who did? Would you call them and check on them more than twice? If you don't know what you would do, or you wouldn't feel comfortable being completely candid and open with your "brothers and sisters in Christ. " I had a man in my Sunday school class who would go on and on and always call me brother in Church, shake my hand, and make one try to feel "brotherly" in church. I haven't heard a word from him or any of the other "brothers in Christ" since D-day. But fortunately, for my sake, there were a few.

    The following Monday, after discovering my affair, I got a couple of phone calls from men who had "heard." If I hadn't received the phone calls, it is very doubtful I would have ever darkened the doors of a

---

[18] Nate Larkin, Samson and the Pirate Monks: Calling Men to Authentic Brotherhood (Nashville, TN: W Pub. Group, 2007).

church ever again; for six days, I shut myself off from God. After D-day, I felt little like praying, and my mother knowing my faith was important to me, would invite me to church, and I would respond, saying that God and I weren't talking right now. I cannot express the magnitude of those men who called me to "check on me" in words. A simple phone call had an immense impact on my life; they said nothing profound; it was just someone exercising love to me when I most needed it. I was down, and I was beaten by my sin, like a dog after scolding who cowers and looks for any sign of recognition. What had been thrown down on my ex-wife and family, expressly how it was falling on them, was cruel beyond measure... I was feeling the guilt both barrels and as precisely as I should. We sometimes have to eat the crap we produce, and I was more than willing for every bite, but with infidelity, those closest to us get the most oversized spoons.

Before D-day, I was reading Thomas Merton's The Seven Storey Mountain. I avoided it several days before reading it. Still, I did, and in there was this *"The truth that many people never understand is that the more you try to avoid suffering, the more you suffer because smaller and more insignificant things start to torture you in proportion to your fear of being hurt."* [19] I began to realize that I had spent my whole life avoiding pain and suffering, and, in this pain, I felt there must be some benefit. I had to lose my fear of the pain because I suspected it would get darker before dawn. I was wallowing in my self-created misery; what I needed was outside myself--I needed a Savior. I had moved out of my parents and into an apartment in the next town over.

I knew the owners of the apartment for almost ten

---

[19] Thomas Merton, The Seven Storey Mountain (San Diego: Harcourt Brace, 1999).

years. They are both highly active in recovery, the man with more than thirty-nine years clean and her with nearly fifteen years. They had contacted me as soon as they heard and offered the apartment with only two conditions: I would be evicted immediately if I "relapsed" and if the woman I had an affair with was ever seen on the property. Words cannot express my gratitude for these people even today; they provided me a safe place for my son and me to rebuild our relationship. They kept a close eye on me but never pried and were always available to talk. They helped and encouraged me during my darkest days, and I will forever be in their gratitude. I don't feel I could adequately repay their love after my ex-wife told me the first time that there was no possibility of reconciliation. I crept back into the darkness of my mind, left the apartment, and wondered about drinking again. At the local grocery store, I found myself sitting in my truck crying, feeling sorry for myself, watching happy couples go in and out of the grocery store. He called and asked me what I was doing and if I was okay. I told him where I was and what I was doing, and he then told me, "Get my butt back home." I did, and we talked; many moments like that make me believe Jesus sent them as guardians to look over me.

I got a part-time job to keep busy and provide financial income to ensure my ex-wife and kids were cared for. Also, I was secretly planning on buying my ex-wife a new wedding band set; staying busy proved vital. It got me out of my head as I would slip into a fantasy land where reconciliation was possible if left to idle thought. I came up with elaborate plans to win her back and save the day (minus the white chariot but close). My landlord would always do his best to keep me grounded, often saying, "women that want to reconcile don't see divorce lawyers." He was right and kept me grounded, but I still reveled in fantasy, which wasn't very healthy for me.

I was alone in my apartment one morning. I was

working from home, and the thought had come over me, and I couldn't shake the feeling of needing to go to the closest church now. It was a Pentecostal church I drove by every day, and COVID-19 had hit only a few weeks before, and I wasn't sure if it was even open. I had become quite familiar with these moments, and in recovery, we call them spiritual experiences or God moments. I knew I had to go to that church, and I had to go right then. I grabbed my shoes and went. I pulled in, and there was a man in there. I frantically knocked on the door, and he begrudgingly opened the door only slightly. I excitedly told him who I was and why I was there and that I had not been to church since the revelation of my affair a few weeks before. I needed to get a church home since I had lost my church home in separation. I talked extremely fast to get everything out because he had yet to open the door fully and only told me that he was the pastor and was on a conference call.

After I told him all I thought he needed to know, he told me they had services next Sunday at 11 a.m., and I was welcome to attend. He shut and locked the door, and I could see him through the window get back to his office. I was a little hurt by his shortness and borderline rudeness after telling him my conviction led to his church door. I stewed on that the rest of the week, but I knew enough never to dismiss a God moment such as I had felt. I was going to have to trust God and roll with it. Moments like that don't happen for no reason. They are usually course corrections, and I have had them before. When I followed them, I always found the Grace of Christ at the other end.

I have also had them and not followed them, and every time pain and suffering followed. That is why I was in the mess I had found myself. I had stopped paying attention to the will of God and stopped listening. Since D-day, I had renewed my faith in God and tried to be the man everyone thought I was. After I ended my affair, I began teaching Sunday school at our church up to the point of the revelation of my affair. I had felt at the time God was allowing me to redeem myself after my infidelities. I can see today he may have been merely building my faith for what was to come or to let me come clean and admit my sins, possibly. I really won't know anything for sure; my guess is merely speculation. My story unfolded the way it did because of my spinelessness, and He will develop the rest for me to show his grace and love.

I went to the Pentecostal Church the following Sunday, and with the COVID-19 crisis in full swing, there was apparent distancing. The Pentecostal preacher said hello and was cordial. With the church being a big part of my family, going back without my family was emotional. I cried the entire service, yet the only one who would speak to me was the preacher. His conversations were surface level and cold despite me telling him the struggles I was having and the need for a Christian community. I went to the next couple of Sundays with no change in the church's openness and welcoming. They were whooping and hollering, praising Jesus but ignoring the crying sinner who sat in the back. Churches are huge on preaching and waving their hands around but disastrously terrible at missions.

When I say missions, I mean amongst themselves; if a church building is needed in a faraway land, such as in Paraguay, or a couple needs money to go on a mission to help those poor people, checks will fly the money will fill the coffers. Everyone feels better for being a better Christian. what about the mission amongst us in our communities. What about the crying grown man in the back who nobody knows? I went to that church every week for a month, and not one person talked to me besides the preacher, and he was doing his duty. I am not critical; I am attempting to be completely candid. I probably had my fair share of opportunities where I ignored the crying dude in the back. I often looked the other way when there were perfect opportunities to carry Christ to others, but I didn't notice, or maybe I didn't want to see. After being the crying dude in the back, I can attest it sucks, and I need to talk about it amongst believers, and I need to do better.

I bounced around several churches over the next couple of months. My crying got less and less, and some churches were very friendly. With the number of churches in the south, one may think it wouldn't be any trouble to find a new church. If I called ten churches, on average, one would answer their phone, and two would return my call. I understand this was at the COVID-19 crisis's height, but not returning phone calls I couldn't understand. I am pretty sure the Pastors of these churches cashed their paychecks. It was beyond frustrating. Why would any organization, business, or group place a phone on their website or have it listed on the internet? Why clearly state they are open for business and not answer their phone and not return phone calls? Sickening is the only word I can describe. I had called around 20 prominent churches in my area, of which I am still waiting for a response. Most eventually called me back some days later; dereliction of duty is the only word I feel is necessary. If it weren't for my ex-wife encouraging me to keep calling the church's again, I would probably still be looking for a church as they seldom took time to respond to my calls or the messages I left.

The church I belong to now, I tried the number several times to no avail and eventually had to email the worship pastor, who then contacted the pastor to contact me in which he did, which proved a blessing. I was desperate for Christian community, and I cannot express my gratitude for his phone call. If you belong to a church, call and email the contact information; please fix it, check if it works. We never know the lives that can be changed and none if they cannot get a hold of us.

After years and years of not feeling like I belonged in a church, I wasn't good enough, and I had to put my best face forward; I realize now how wrong I was. I can belong to any body of believers I have a purpose, I am a sinner, a drunk lustful adulterer, and in many people's eyes, that's all I will ever be. I messed up not just once but many times in the age of Facebook and social media. We must always present ourselves in the perfect light. I am not a faithful man; that's because I need a savior. I always seem to do the wrong thing. I am surprised by the number of people who refused to speak to me, as I have known them for years. I know perfectly well they stumbled, and I went to great lengths to help them up. That doesn't matter because they are at a loss, not because they are no longer in my life, but I could see people in their true light.

They are cheating themselves out of the experience of forgiveness. I heard a recovery speaker one time tell his story. In his story was severe sexual abuse from his childhood that he had thought he had controlled it enough where it didn't bother him. He shared that he heard a fifth step (confession) from one of the men he was working with. The man out of the blue told him in strict confidence that he had touched a young nephew inappropriately, he next said in what seemed like an eternity. Still, he immediately went into a whole circuit of emotions while this man was dumping his guts to him. He confessed to going from rage and wanting to attack him to fear, then sadness, and then the warmness of his creator came over him. He thought this man is a child of God just as I am imperfect as Jesus, and I have forgiven him; why can't I? There weren't many dry eyes in the church basement that night after he spoke; it was beyond moving. I wish I could love people as he has.

In His grace, I believe God has used my addictions to crush my superficiality and surface-level faith and force me to accept the Gospel. I cannot change what I did; I still have spells that I hate myself for what I have done and loath my existence for the damage it has done to my daughter immensely. I can only change what I do from D-day and forward. I cannot live fully; I need strong people to help me. I need a genuine and honest community. I have to surround myself with those I can be sincere with because I am a sinner, and I believe I can keep my promises when I am willing to do the right thing. I am rewarded with an inner peace that no external stimulus can produce. When I am unwilling to do the right thing, I become restless, irritable, and discontent; the choice is always mine.

# 9 SHAME ON YOU

*"There is no birth of consciousness without pain."* - Carl Jung

During the initial months of the COVID-19 scare, I was three and a half months post-D-day and still attempting to secure a church home. My ex-wife had observed many times while I was in church during our marriage that I was too open about my struggles with sin when I spoke in Sunday school and that it wasn't a recovery meeting. As she put it, "church people don't talk like that" my response was always that "church people" should be more open and honest with each other as they are in recovery rooms. I feel that way even more, so it is freeing and exhilarating to have all your secrets out. I admit that enthusiasm to tell others openly and honestly about what God has helped you overcome should come with a discretion that I haven't always implemented as much as I should have. My reckless openness to people has led to many disheartening conversations that have discouraged me about organized religion. I know now that it isn't their fault at all, but maybe it is the message. I heard a quote from Gregg Popovich, Coach of the San Antonio Spurs, *"The measure of who we are is how we react to something that doesn't go our way."* I believe I have the right message and would be excited to share myself amenably and honestly. When I did not hear the responses I wanted to hear, I shut down like a child. With awareness of facts about ourselves always comes with responsibilities;

I had one heck of a time getting churches to call me back during the COVID scare if I wanted to know information. If I called ten churches, maybe four or fewer would answer. I had one church in particular not too far from the apartment I was living in and on the way to my part-time job. I called them, left a voicemail, and was shocked that the church secretary called me back within two hours. I was delighted to return her phone call. She was a pleasant woman and a delight to speak with, but I began to share more than I should have as I warmed up in the conversation. I began to communicate openly and honestly that I was looking for a church home because I was going through a divorce instead of leaving my response at a surface level. She asked explicitly why so, and I just told her it was because I had an affair with a woman I met in recovery, and I lost my ex-wife of twenty years. Her response was a simple "Shame on you."

With her response, we both were silent for some time until I responded, "Why would you say that to me?"

She replied coldly, "Because you ought not to have done that."

And then I told her, "I know that, and I will pay for it dearly, and I am doing my best to recover and make it right. I do not need your shame, I have enough, so I say to you, 'Shame on you, dear ma'am.'"

She apologized politely, and the rest of the conversation was us re-establishing the dialogue to a graceful and non-personal level. I admired her elegance and sense of politeness; I did my utmost to convey my gratitude to her, and we ended the call on good terms.

First Corinthians 16:13 tells us to *"Be on guard. Stand firm in the faith. Be courageous. Be strong."* With the gift of self-reflection, I learned in the recovery rooms that I have had considerable time to break down this conversation in my head and pick it apart honestly and with much thought. My first response was regret that I said anything to the woman; I should have taken it and moved on. *"But false niceness can never and will never produce an authentic, deeply meaningful relationship, just like weeds won't magically produce zinnias,"* [20]says Paul Coughlin in his book, No More Christian Nice Girl: When Just Being Nice—Instead of Good—Hurts You, Your Family, and Your Friends. I don't regret rectifying her in the least, and I believe her response, while loving and cordial, is why I am writing this book, and that is why I am going to devote an entire chapter to such.

The painful emotional feeling of humiliation and distress caused by my infidelity discovery has been my constant companion since D-day; it has consumed me entirely. Even months later, after my open admission of my infidelities, I appear shy and shameful around those I have openly and willingly confessed my past transgressions. I avoid women because there must be something inside that many women can associate with the pain. As I have shared my story with others, I am amazed by how many lives have been affected by infidelity. The common factor is the same; pornography has touched their lives negatively in some way. We are as sick as our own secrets, and one upside is, I have no secrets anymore. I have nothing to lose sharing my story with others but the shame that is covering me. Haunted by my feelings of unworthiness and shame, would I allow the darkness to overcome me? Or will I let Jesus guide me and direct me and stay in the fight?

I am compelled to write this book, and I feel it was a spiritual experience that propelled me. I was wallowing in my bed, feeling sorry for myself as usual and overcome with the urge to write. I got up that morning and have worked on it ever since. The pain I created and

---

[20] Paul Coughlin, "No More Christian Nice Girl Quotes by Paul Coughlin," Goodreads (Goodreads), accessed February 16, 2021, https://www.goodreads.com/work/quotes/7285633-no-more-christian-nice-girl-when-just-being-nice--instead-of-good--hurt.

the agony I have passed off to my family are all a waste if it doesn't lead to my humility. Despite how painful it may be, I need to reveal
the real me to others. There will be judgment, and there will be shame; as Popeye said, *"I am what I am."* In my open admission of my shortcoming and struggle with sin, I believe the power of my story. I don't care anymore. I have lost my ex-wife of twenty years for my submission to my sin, and my daughter won't talk to me; I have nothing to lose.

A man backed up to a cliff has two options, fight or jump, and I am not jumping, not today. Just as Job, who was faithful as I wasn't, in Job 1:21, says, *"Naked I came from my mother's womb, and naked I will depart. The Lord gave, and the Lord has taken away; may the name of the Lord be praised" (NIV).* Any status I thought I had before D-day was nothing, but with what the Lord had provided, and I didn't take care of it, and I rightly lost it. The Lord will give, and he will take. I must humble myself and be myself, especially in God; He sees everything anyway.

Shame tells me I am not good enough; shame tells me I must put on my mask and appear like everyone else. I used to love getting drunk Sunday morning and pretending I was fishing; there was one place I would go. I would see all the clean-cut, respectable church folk with their perfect families walk into a local Baptist church as I swilled my morning beer and vodka. I would look at them with disgust and contempt because I felt so inferior. I wanted to be happy like they appeared to be. Shame was talking to me then and held me back. Matthew, the tax collector, was cut out from Jewish society because of his profession; he was profiteering off the Jewish people. He wasn't allowed near the temple or any of the synagogues, yet Jesus chose him.

Matthew 9:9-13 states, *"As Jesus passed on from there,*

*he saw a man called Matthew sitting at the tax booth, and he said to him, 'Follow me.' And he rose and followed him. And as Jesus reclined at table in the house, behold, many tax collectors and sinners came and were reclining with Jesus and his disciples. And when the Pharisees saw this, they said to his disciples, 'Why does your teacher eat with tax collectors and sinners?' But when he heard it, he said, 'Those who are well have no need of a physician, but those who are sick. Go and learn what this means: "I desire mercy, and not sacrifice." For I came not to call the righteous, but sinners'" (ESV).*

You can be a person who does no wrong your entire life and yet be a horrible person. The absence of bad doesn't automatically mean good. God alone knows our heart; we cannot view the outside and bypass the heart. Avoiding bad isn't the only goal; do I truly seek to be good for the sake alone of being closer to Christ. My motives are always my litmus test; I must actively self-reflect and test my actions and thoughts daily. In them, I see I am no better than anyone. The shame we feel from the flock may very well be a corrupt flock who is only clean outside.

I don't feel any shame when I pray with Jesus; I know He accepts my brokenness if I am honest with Him. If I don't feel shame in the presence of Jesus, why do I continue to feel indignity around others? That woman at the church, I have to say, meant no harm. She was doing well what she thought was right traditionally. Churches are very shaming; I guess that is how to keep their masses in line. I believe it just drives sinful behavior underground; even before my infidelity was discovered in my marriage, the congregation would learn of adultery, and the couple would split. The offending party was never seen in those church doors ever again. I can see now clearly more so than ever facing those from your church are the hardest people to face. Jesus never shamed anyone, but the religious elite of his day certainly did.

He loved Sinners and made sure he was amongst them. He was eating with the tax collectors and the sinners; the tax collectors were the considered enemy of the Jewish people. Jesus being seen amid those considered the enemy of God's chosen people was similar to Billy Graham having tea and crumpets with Al Qaeda. The tax collectors were more despised than the Romans and justly so. After D-day, I had found a part-time job, and occasionally, I would bump into members of my church. I would make complete eye contact, so I knew they saw me, and then I could see the shock on their faces as they recognized me; watching them turn the other way was always the most hurtful.

That was the most hurtful, seeing the people I went to church with and even taught in my Sunday school class. I would see them week after week professing their love of Christ and committing to the church yet turn away from me. It was more hurtful than those I didn't go to church with, even if I knew they were believers and related to them. They would ignore me or look away when they saw me. With social media, Facebook, especially keeping the impression of perfection and others' lives to envy, has been a great narcotic of the masses. To find those worthy of shame and discuss their misdeeds amongst those closest to us, I cannot think of any other type of ego-boosting exercise than to slander others upon discovering their misgivings and conduct deviates from proper social behavior. I talk of intolerance; while I was intolerant, I missed the forest's reality and beauty because some of its trees' ugliness diverted me.

I have succumbed to that temptation on more than one occasion, and I know for myself it was always to distract from my insecurities. If I could put someone else down, I would lift myself. As Jesus said in Matthew 7:3-5, *"Why do you look at the speck of sawdust in your brother's eyes and pay no attention to the plank in your own eye? How can you say to your brother, let me take the speck out of your eye when all the time there is a plank in your own eye? You hypocrite, first take the plank out of your own eye, and then you will see clearly to remove the speck from your brother's eye" (NIV).*

I believe now; shame kills people if someone has succumbed to sin and is killing our church. In the immediate months following D-day, shame was my constant companion; I had so much trouble seeing beyond it. It was and still is my constant companion; my sin has destroyed my family and is the single-handed reason my marriage of twenty years ended. My children's lives are forever altered, and the shame of my actions has been thrust upon them. The pride they once had that I was their dad had been substituted by scorn and embarrassment. It is doubtful I will ever have a relationship with my only daughter ever again—due to the revelation of my unfaithfulness to her mother. And the shattering of her image of me beyond providential intervention seems remote.

Adversity indeed introduces us to ourselves like nothing else—the sideways glances from brothers and sisters in Christ. The quick detours in my presence by those with whom only weeks before I sang hymns of praise in church. The silence from those once close to you doesn't serve any purpose that I can immediately see and only seems to show me the errors of my past judgment of others and how wrong I was.

*"Real freedom is freedom from the opinions of others. Above all, freedom from your opinions about yourself."*[21]— Brennan Manning, The Wisdom of Tenderness: What Happens When God's Fierce Mercy Transforms Our Lives.

---

[21] Brennan Manning, The Wisdom of Tenderness: What Happens When God's Fierce Mercy Transforms Our Lives, Amazon (HarperSanFrancisco, 2004), https://www.amazon.com/Wisdom-Tenderness-Happens-Fierce-Transforms/dp/0060724463.

I'm compelled to share my story for no other reason than to broadcast my errors and to show the love God has shown me through others. Also, the detestation that because of my sin, both have been for a purpose.

I was amazed two months after the revelation of my infidelity. The one person who had the most reason in this world to hate me looked at me and said that she forgave me and didn't hate me. That was harder to hear than if she cussed me out. Of all the people in the world to hate me for what I have done, she had every reason, but she doesn't. She has in many ways exhibited more love and forgiveness to me in our interactions since D-day. And this is simply unbelievable to me. She was the lubricant for me to get my son and me moving on our relationship rebuilding. Our relationship has been mature and cordial due to her forgiveness.

Shame is pity turned inwards, and shame in its proper place is practical but only within its lifecycle. The paradox of shame is the lack of shame when sin is revealed. It can lead to arrogance and putting the blame where it shouldn't be.

On the other side of the spectrum, a surplus of shame can prove fatal, leading regretfully to suicide. Not being able to see beyond the shame of wallowing in past misery can hinder us from God's love. Just as grieving is a process, so shame also a process. Love and forgiveness from others that matter can shine the light to the exit, but we must never forget. We don't deserve others' forgiveness.

Matthew 6:14-15 tells us, *"For if you forgive other people when they sin against you, your heavenly Father will also forgive you. But if you do not forgive others their sins, your Father will not forgive your sins" (NIV)*. I must forgive quickly for me to be forgiven and not lull myself into victimization and enablement of a cycle of judging others for their reaction to the wrongs I have done. To crawl out of the pit of shame I have dug by my actions, I must love others regardless of reciprocal love.

In many ways, shame is our realization that we are not the hero in our own story we tell ourselves. When we come clean about our true nature, we cannot help but realize we are the villain or even the clown in our story. If our shame gets misplaced, someone close to us should attempt to readjust our shame and put it back where it belongs. We aren't helpful with too much shame; we need others to love and rescue us from the bottomless pit of shame. I had a neighbor, and I looked up to him; he is a good man; his wife is a great woman. One of the first times I went to my house after D-day, the neighbors were in the yard. They wouldn't look at me, of course, and in my mind, they were judging me. A week or two later, he saw me again and approached me. I couldn't remember everything he said as I just started balling and saying how sorry I was. But I know he told me I was still a good man. He loved me doing that and was trying to help me in my shame, and I will forever be in his gratitude. It took courage to come to talk to me and say the things he said I didn't deserve. I needed to hear from a man, mostly that I wasn't all bad; what I did was terrible, indeed, but my sin must not define my future.

Shame is useful; without shame, we cannot feel the total weight of our sin. If we never felt the shame, we would repeat the same sins over and over. Christ Jesus said in John 8:33, *"Ye shall know the truth, and the truth shall make you free" (NIV)*. Shame reveals the truth to us and forces us to feel just a little of the pain we spread to our loved ones. I must feel the pain of my sin; there must be consequences for my drifting from the sunlight of the spirit. I purposely broke a firmly rooted commitment that held my family together for purely selfish reasons and did it in secret. Shame and time in honest reflection have afforded me the blessed opportunity to unravel the total amount of pain I have caused. I grasp that I cannot feel what those affected by my sin, but I am willing to go to any lengths to ease their pain and help heal.

In Dante's Inferno, the fourteenth-century epic poem follows Dante, the main character, which traverses through hell. He categorized hell into nine circles of hell, ranging from the first circle (limbo) containing the unbaptized and virtuous pagans. They did not accept Christ, although not sinful enough to warrant damnation. To in order Lust, Gluttony, Greed, Wrath, Heresy, Violence, Fraud, and the lowest circle of hell being Treachery. Dante's central character notion was that the worst of all moral behavior is treachery, to betray others' trust.

In contrast, this is not a biblical reference at all but isn't without merit. Infidelity is a form of treason because it betrays the trust in the marriage and the core family unit. This is what sustains long-term peaceful growth and collaboration in the family unit. My actions undermined my children's faith in the institution of marriage. I have not only robbed them of their core family. I have completely changed how they see the world.

How can my daughter or son ever look at a supposed married man and not doubt the validity of his faithfulness? If their father was unfaithful, why wouldn't anyone else? Their necessary faith in life has been rocked to the very core. They will doubt every relationship to protect themselves from being hurt again. I have distorted how my children view the world, and worse, made them bitter; that's what Satan does. Upon great reflection on Dante's Inferno, betrayal is the lowest form of hell brought on others. In the divine comedy, the Devil was in the ninth level, surrounded by those who betrayed others' trust.

That woman at the church didn't need to shame me; I needed love. I openly confessed my sins to her because I knew concealing my sins lead me back into that life of secrecy. Jesus loved sinners and rebuked those in authority who passed judgment on them. Paradoxically, he was quick to point out the sins of those who he had come across. Jesus loved like no other and still does but uses our brokenness, loves the sinner. Peter's betrayal of his master Jesus three times was foretold to Peter at the last supper, of which he didn't believe he was capable. How often have I looked upon others and thought to myself, no way, I would never. But in reality, my correct response should be, I pray not, or by God's grace, there go I.

Jesus uses our brokenness just as he used Peter's moral relapse and his refusal of grace to show his love. We all stumble in the perfect world of Facebook, and other media straying from polite communal norms enact others to rebuke us quickly. Sadly, that is also in our church; it turns everyone into liars and counterfeit. We conceal our sin until it is too late and comes out in more damaging ways to everyone. Everything has consequences, and what I did to my family has serious consequences. And I will be making amends and attempting to repair the damage I had done. Sin always has effects, and shame is helpful to a point. After Jesus had risen from the dead, he loved Peter and used his sin to his glory in asking him to feed his sheep. Everything is used for good in this world, even sin. And when we repent and try to correct our misgivings, which is where the true love of Christ comes.

I cannot and must never talk about a body of believers or anyone, as I learned in recovery years ago. And I will always keep my faith in the first person. I have sinned so much, and even now, after D-Day, I am nowhere close to where I ought to be; I fail so much. I know I am nowhere near where I deserve to be. I am right where God has me. Shame is mighty. I have told my ex-wife with tear-filled eyes that I would give everything I have and ever have to take their pain away. And I meant it with every fiber of being in me when I said it. I have exposed myself to writing this book and revealing my failings as a husband, father, man, and Christian. I am not naïve and know some may use this information to gossip and smear my trampled name to elevate themselves. I don't give a damn. I am sorry beyond words for what I have done to my family, and I will always feel shame for that. I don't believe it will ever go away, and I don't want it to because I cannot forget. As it says in Proverbs 6:32-33, *"But a man who commits adultery has no sense; whoever does so destroys himself. Blows and disgrace are his lots, and his shame will never be wiped away" (NIV)*. I have been forgiven more than I deserve, but I must never forget and try to use this shame for good.

We are a product of our mistakes; I must accept that the most crucial thing about regret is that it is useless. The only value of it is the lessons I have learned, and passing those lessons on to someone else is crucial. The entire Bible is full of fallible people, from the first true human, Cain, to Paul. They all were sinful and disobedient to God in one way or another. In one sense, the Bible is a lesson learned manual for the deviation of God's will. King David, who was no angel, was called a man after God's own heart. He dealt with his fair share of shame and regret, but it didn't deter him from learning from his mistakes and passing those lessons onto others.

What if I can get this book into the hands of a man who is struggling like I was? Armed with my story, he may not want to put his family through the pain mine had felt. And just maybe, it gives him the courage to be completely honest with someone about his sin and addictions, and in doing this, it saves his family. It will also urge a church group or body of believers to put their masks down enough to be vulnerable to love the sinners despite social norms. That would be beautiful and worth a shot to convert my constant companion of shame into grace. I miss my family and miss my daughter. I know now I didn't love them the way they deserved, so I lost them, but just maybe I can, with this book, help my children convert their shame of me to the pride that I am their Dad.

## 10 MORNING AFTER PILL

After my separation, I worked at a pharmacy and convenience store to fill my time and keep my mind occupied. It proved a blessing, as the money sustained me, ensuring my wife and kids were minimally affected. As a store clerk, I stocked shelves, ran the register, cleaned the bathrooms, and filled the cooler. Working with the public was challenging. As a Christian, I shuddered at the thought of stocking shelves with Morning after pill contraceptives. At times I would knock them over or hide them. If I were reprimanded, I would congratulate myself because I felt this was my Christian duty.

I remember a young lady at the register who looked embarrassed and never made eye contact. She was purchasing Plan B morning-after pill contraceptive. I looked her over, made eye contact, and then walked away, refusing to sell her the Morning after pill. I was full of self-righteous intoxication. I walked around the store, puffing my chest out like I had done my Christian duty. I even went and found some company for my rationalization. I talked to a fellow employee to whom I promptly apologized for not ringing that woman up. She said she understood because she knew I was religious.

With that validation firmly planted in my mind, I went home with my chest puffed out that I had done my Christian duty and stood up for my beliefs. I was filled with the intoxicating rush as though I had stood for my faith. It was a temporary high. Without my family, I am more aware of what is happening in my life, with a considerable increase in time reflecting on my daily actions. How often are we the hero in our own story when we should be the villain? And even sometimes the buffoon. I began to think of what happened from a different angle. Self-reflection has become a blessing; I began to self-reflect on the situation over and over in my head. Second Corinthians 13:5 says, *"Examine yourselves, to see whether you are in the faith. Test yourselves. Or do you not realize this about yourselves, that Jesus Christ is in you? —unless indeed you fail to meet the test!" (ESV)*.

The following day on my morning commute, the entire story changed; I was telling myself. What about the girl? I remembered every detail about her in my head. She was mainly wearing the look she gave me as we made eye contact for a brief second, and I walked away. I failed the test when I was rallying myself as the hero in my own story for over twelve hours when I was the villain. My self-righteous arrogance blinded me; I failed to see the vital point of the lesson. I destroyed my family because of my sin, and I suddenly wanted to become uppity and self-righteous. Who am I to judge anyone for anything? I do not know that young women's story, and if I suddenly want to become "churchy," especially after all the whining and self-loathing I had been doing about people not loving me, and here I do the same thing.

If someone is purchasing pills such as that, their life may have negative consequences, and the proper time to act religious has long passed. There is a process to everything; people are extraordinarily complicated. With anything, timing is everything. And with spiritual maturity, we learn when and where to do things; nobody knew better than Jesus. In John 4, when Jesus confronts the Samaritan woman at the well, he was not fazed by her sin and didn't confront her right away with her sin; he shared the good news he brought first that he offered her water in which she wouldn't thirst Again. The Samaritan woman is poor and an outcast; even among the outcasts, the Samaritans and Jesus still took her time. He never strayed away from anyone willing to accept him.

I am grossly underqualified to pass judgment on anyone; I was blind to my actions in many ways or wasn't fully accepting my actions' repercussions, which had blinded me. What I do as a result of the revealing of our sin speaks louder than any sermon because that is Christ's redemption. Christ's redemption doesn't prevent us from paying the consequences for our sin. I had caused significant and very much lasting adverse effects on those closest to me. They get the most giant bites of the crap I dealt out.

I used this analogy many times to people I worked with in recovery over my many years, and I am not sure if it helped anyone. When we are trapped in sin and destroying people's lives, we are putting big piles of crap right at their feet. Our sin and betrayal stink up their existence. Once we stop doing the offensive behavior, the accumulation of crap doesn't magically disappear like in some magical Christian miracle, forgiven by Christ, and they may even forgive us. But that big stinking pile of crap is still left there. If left, the flies come, and it's much worse. The deal is they get to throw that crap right back at you whenever they want and however they choose.

That is the healing we cannot get all holier than thinking I can avoid the crap I left in everyone's life. It is my crap that is being thrown, and if I don't like it, I shouldn't put any more crap in their pile. Each person my actions have negatively affected has a pile. Some may not want to throw their crap right away; they may want to let it fester and get wretched. It's their choice; it's their pile, and I put it there. If ever they want to throw it at me, I must find the courage to take it. I may try to initiate someone to start throwing and adding to the pile unintentionally. I have been reminded of my analogy dealing with the fallout of my sin. The most courageous act is a closed mouth and open ears. They may be wrong in what they say, but so what. It's the emotions the offended party needs to get it out; they have earned that right by my actions.

The details don't matter, but faith is most tested

because of pride. Our already smeared name doesn't matter; we must stop adding to the pile. Eventually, with courage and humility, the piles will go down of those that choose to throw. If I don't like it, I shouldn't have put crap at those feet. We must take our licks and shut our mouths; once your name is mud, no sense in proving everyone right by acting like a hurt fool. There is no sense in me ever thinking I am anything more than what I truly am, and that is a sinner of the worst kind.

*"But for the grace of God, there go I"* was a phrase I heard echoed throughout the rooms of recovery. As Galatians 6:3-4 says, *"If anyone thinks they are something when they are not, they deceive themselves. Each one should test their own actions. Then they can take pride in themselves alone, without comparing themselves to someone else" (NIV).* I cannot help but be grateful for the humiliation resulting from the sin that has forced me to my knees to understand the pain I have caused. I am what I have done, not what my ego tells me. My shame has thrust the feeling upon me, but I cannot forget as I work to subside the crippling of shame. I must say to myself the correct story I cannot, once the smoke is clear, put my halo on and shadow over the past at the detriment of the present.

Thomas Merton once said, *"A saint is not someone who is good, but who experiences the goodness of God."* [22]The very minute I forget how much worse I deserve and how many blessings he has bestowed on me, I will tend to forget how deeply loved I am by Jesus. There are many things in my life; I have earned degrees, medals, accolades, and such. If I am genuinely humble, it is because I have been given so much. I have hands to work, a mind to think, and even my talents to capitalize on for financial gain. I have been given

---

[22] Merton, Thomas. The Seven Storey Mountain. San Diego: Harcourt Brace, 1999.

life itself by my creator. When I look back at my life, I can see his hand in all things, even when I wasn't speaking with him. I can see his handiwork in the ups and the downs.

Even with my alcoholism and sexual addictions, he was like the vigilant lifeguard keeping watch over me, so I didn't stray too far into deep water. He made sure I was struggling enough to remember but not forget it. I am amazed at how much I learned about myself and how much of a better man I am since the day before I sobered up on December 19, 2005. In hindsight, I can see that I only learn through pain. I wish it weren't so, but it is; I must do better. I can recollect with honest reflection how many times it must have God looking out for me. The more than can be accurately counted is his grace in my life, driving drunk, blacking out while driving, and not remembering how I got where I was and why. I had woken up early one morning with my truck neatly nestled between two trees off I-95 in Rhode Island. A slight hill had stopped my vehicle; an inch or two, either way, could have proven fatal. The bushes had concealed my truck from the road. There are countless stories such as that I cannot explain why I was not maimed or killed or, even worse, and I could have hurt so many people.

I must stay honest and tell my story. The humiliation from D-day and afterward forced me to get honest about something in my life I was hiding and lacked the bravery to divulge myself. We are sick as our secrets, and it is freeing to know I have no more secrets. Keeping the spiritual trajectory that my sin had humbled me to must remain to ease resolution as much as possible with those I hurt most. They must see the change in me, not only in my words. As Stephen Covey says, *"You can't talk your way out of problems you behaved yourself into."*[23] The biggest deceptions I have ever done in my life have been with myself. My behavior must match my words in all things, even when nobody is looking.

Honesty, openness, and willingness to accept and seek my savior's will, I have heard so many churchy talks from others and, most notably, myself. I taught Sunday school while concealing in secret the affair in my marriage. I would think sometimes and look at the people in my Sunday school "if they knew who I was, they wouldn't speak to me," and in almost all cases, it was true some of those who I held hands with and prayed with and simply looked the other way if they saw me which was very hurtful. That doesn't matter at all; I am entirely responsible for everything that happens to me. I am responsible not for others' actions but my reaction to their actions. I am accountable.

I am an honest man because I have surrounded myself with authentic people who are not scared of the truth despite how ugly that may be. I cannot and must not be the only guardian of my story. Even Jesus sent the apostles out in groups to carry the message of salvation and ensure the story of Jesus is passed correctly. I have to stick with the winners. It is tough to find such men, especially in a church where the church mask portrays the best possible image and is not tempted not to lie about one's true self, not to tarnish Christianity's image. Even as adults, the old advice is accurate *"show me your friends, and I will show you your future."* The Christians we hang around are the Christians we become; for the average church-attending person, there is no immediate natural consequence to not pushing the spiritual envelope.

For myself, it can prove fatal as you have read throughout this book; you can see when I have not

---

[23] Stephen R. Covey, The 7 Habits of Highly Effective People (London: Simon & Schuster UK Ltd., 2020).

diligently and fervently aligned my will to that of God's, my narcissist childish self slowly takes over. My sincere desire that anyone reading this can see themselves even a little in my story and hopefully give them the courage to be more open and honest within their church. My very life depends on my relationship with Jesus and my association with positive people. All I have is a daily reprieve based solely on my spiritual condition. A day at a time mentality I learned in recovery years ago must still be enforced.

Keeping the flame alive must be kindled by a steady diet of scripture. Before D-day, I only read enough scripture to get by, and I can see now that didn't work as it eventually led to Satan taking advantage of my lax Christianity and, like a stubborn sticker, peeled a little at a time. My routines keep me sane. I keep experimenting with making them achievable and practical. I can have the most robust church, pastor, men, accountability partners, ad infinitum. But if I do not practice my relationship with Christ alone when nobody is around, it is all for naught; everything else we do in our faith is secondary to our time alone with Christ. Jesus himself went off and spent time with his father, and he made it a priority.

Why would I think that a church, preacher, the congregation would draw me closer to Christ if I do not spend time? Daniel 6:10 tells us that Daniel prayed three times a day. Psalm 119:164 says King David praised God for his righteousness seven times a day. The Jewish prayer schedule was once in the morning, around midday. In the evening, I am reading about increasing my walk with Christ. Taking five to ten minutes several times in my life could reveal any downside. I have been doing just that for several months and have done more to raise my God consciences' than anything I have done before. I heard on a Duck Dynasty podcast to always travel with a Bible "to ensure you are always adequately armed." I had thought it silly, but the mere fact of ensuring I always had a physical Bible close has helped me on several occasions to stop and read a little scripture and remind myself what I am trying to accomplish.

Sometimes, for me, the physical act is far more important than the spiritual connection. The old analogy of "Ninety percent of success is just showing up." I believe to be honest with my relationship with Jesus, as you have already read. I bring no specific spiritual talents. I am a filthy sinner of the lowest caliber. If I cannot get to a better relationship with Jesus with some enlightenment with theological realization, blind grunt power and repetition will have to do. I have heard memorizing Bible verses works as well, and I am trying that. But just like the Pharisees who had learned large tracts of scripture, we can have all the book knowledge, but without humility, it's for naught. I keep trying new things to strengthen my relationship with Jesus. What may work for someone may not work for me if I keep myself honest and bounce my true story against someone else.

In recovery, for many years, I heard it said, "It's an inside job," meaning with faith, our relationship must be from within ourselves. All the fancy stuff on the outside can be a self-proclaimed religious honcho if I cannot be honest with God. I believe this is the best definition of humility... I must be myself all the time and drop all the false bravado and pride, especially in front of Jesus. Galatians 6:3-5 says, *"If anyone thinks they are something when they are not, they deceive themselves. Each one should test their own actions. Then they can take pride in themselves alone, without comparing themselves to someone else, for each one should carry their own load" (NIV).*

I must test my own stories and try every day to be as close to what I genuinely am in front of others. I am nobody special, but I am sincere. It pains me to think of the hurt I put on others simply because I was selfish;

others have paid the most for my sin. Some will forgive me; others won't; Jesus has already paid for my sins, and he has forgiven me, but I must never forget.

I am a sinner, but I can and must change if my relationship with Jesus is right; my life seems to flow not smoothly but flows with a purpose. Purpose means my actions are genuinely for something besides serving myself. A life revolving around the pursuit of self is never a life well-lived.

Love others, trust God, and help someone else was a mantra often expressed in recovery rooms. Many of the sayings I heard were often repeated in recovery while not necessarily biblical but biblical in principles and based on substantial experience that everyone could use. As Thomas Merton said, *"The beginning of love is the will to let those we love be perfectly themselves, the resolution not to twist them to fit our own image."*[24] I have spent too much time trying to change people to suit me instead of loving them as Christ loved us.

I was talking with a man after Bible study this week. After discussing my difficulties with porn and alcoholism, he secretly confided in me his past problems with gambling. This was after many conversations with him and me, confiding fully in him and to the group. He trusted me enough to share that with me. I was flattered, but I looked at him and asked him why he didn't share that with others. He simply didn't have an answer as to why he hasn't. In reflection, I remember being in church for many years, and I always thought I was no good, and I went underground. I was looking at porn every night, and my marriage was eroding. When I would go to church, everyone was smiling and happy. I thought, why am I so

---

[24] Merton, Thomas. The way of Chuang Tzu. New York: Random House, 1992.

dysfunctional, why am I so weak? I have accepted Christ as them, and I tithe; I do everything I am supposed to; why am I such a loser?

I can see how it was all a mirage, a church fairy tale; everyone struggles in one shape or form from one extreme to the other. Brennan Manning said, *"In a futile attempt to erase our past, we deprive the community of our healing gift. If we conceal our wounds out of fear and shame, our inner darkness can neither be illuminated nor become a light for others."* [25] I can easily take the time and heal my sin's effects and lull into a nice Christian guy again. It's effortless to play like everything is nice and peachy. I become very much like an actor trying to arrange

a show and present myself in an adequate light in front of my audience.

As damaging as it was and still is to my family, my past is absolutely a gift. I am eternally grateful for the lessons I have learned about living life on life's terms. Many of the Bible characters' fallibility is because they struggle with the same things, especially Samson and King David; their struggles with lust and women are well known. The difference between Samson and Kind David is admission and friends. David always had Jonathan by his side; Samson lone wolfed it. The entire book of Psalms reeks of King David's failings as a man and as king. He published it and made sure everyone knew what a screwup he was, and in doing so, he showed how great God was. Samson never admitted his faults. We are as sick as our secrets, and fortunately, I have no more secrets. And I have every intention of keeping it that way; living with a secret is no life at all. In my continued open admission, I hope and pray to keep earning the trust of other men to

---

[25] Brennan Manning, John Blase, and Jonathan Foreman, Abba's Child: the Cry of the Heart for Intimate Belonging (Colorado Springs, CO: NavPress, 2015).

admit their sin openly. This facilitates healing and is the beacon in the darkness. When we lower ourselves so others can honestly see us, we cannot help but bring glory to God, but only if we are no longer trapped in the sin.

Could you imagine a place where you could praise God without fear of ridicule? If you had doubts, anxiety, and sins to discuss, you could easily find a trusted companion or even your church leadership. If they couldn't help you, they would help you get the help you needed. A body of believers of Christ keeps what is said in that church body in the strictest confidence. You have full knowledge that others in the church have struggled and are sinners down and dirty as you.

I do not know where I am going and what the future holds for me, I cannot see the road ahead of me, but I must follow the path that lays ahead of me. If I stay on course and fill my desire to please Him in all I do, I believe my route will be graced by the mere fact of my desire to please Him. I pray I have the strength to move forward living as He would want me to, forgoing all earthly desires. Most days, I am afraid and doubting my future; my faithful resolution is only when I am alone with Him. I often feel lost and desolate, but I must not fear as He is never far away. I must remain willing to face the perils ahead. May God please bless those I have hurt and only help me to the effect that it is helpful to do His will, never mine.

# 11 THE DEVIL AMONGST US

Even Job, one of the holiest of men ever to have lived, had to make a covenant with God with his eyes. Job 31:1 (NIV) says, *"I made a covenant with my eyes not to look lustfully at a young woman."* I have heard it said our eyes are like rifle sights; what we look at is what we are hunting. We look at what we desire; we can proclaim anything with our lips, but we want it despite our declarations if we are looking at it. Our eyes are the pathway to our heart, and what we put our eyes on will fill our hearts, despite anything we say or feel. If Job knew this several thousand years ago, why are we still struggling with this today with our porn-induced society? His wisdom rings even more valid today.

Have you ever wondered why it considered "normal" in today's world to watch fake people having fake sex while masturbating to it? Porn is a weapon; porn is mostly free because you are the product. Porn destroys marriages, families, relationships, and love. Intimacy, as intended by God, becomes out of reach.

People that watch porn at least once a month:
- 64% of Christian men, and,
- 15% of Christian women

Church pastors using porn regularly and currently struggling:
- 1 in 5 youth pastors use porn regularly, and,
- 1 in 7 senior pastors uses porn regularly.

That is more than 50,000 U.S. church leaders.[i]

The devil is amongst us, and his face is porn, and it has infiltrated our homes, marriages, and churches. The shame of porn causes its silence, which facilities it as the silent killer. Pornography has become a hidden, invisible plaque and has trapped many good men and women and destroys our families.

How much porn is being viewed by all men in our church? If we swapped the name porn with beer, you could bet we would be more open to discussing it. Concerned wives and family members would add their struggling spouses to all the prayer lists they could find and certainly would be discussed more quickly than when a spouse knows her husband has become dependent on pornography to function. We might forget eighty years ago, it was taboo to discuss one's struggle with liquor, and maybe twenty years ago, drugs held the same clout. Shame and secrecy have blocked those who are afflicted from the sunlight of God. Online pornography is one of the devil's greatest weapons to destroy. Its most remarkable attribute is the cycle of shame. Viewing porn causes shame, which leads to isolation. Then isolation leads to a lot of negative emotional states like loneliness and anger. These and other "triggers" make a person vulnerable to pornography, and the cycle starts all over again.

Man's most destructive weapon ever created is arguably the atomic bomb. I believe it pales compared to online pornography with its lethality to humanity. Could one imagine us dropping a nuclear weapon on a country, and everyone was so ashamed they refused to tell anyone and went to great lengths to conceal the bomb blast? The entire nation could be destroyed, and not a single cry for help would be uttered before it is too late. We could look back with wonder and astonishment and puzzlement as to why. That's what porn does to our lives; it destroys—it never builds. Its rapacious appetite is never quenched. It is like a hurricane with no end in sight, blowing through destroying everything it touches. I can almost guarantee every person knows someone who is struggling with pornography at some level. You work with them, are related to them, go to church with them, and don't even know it. It is a time for transparency and to claim the monster in the closet.

With every fiber in my being, I believe without porn, my marriage and my family would still be together. Pornography warped my mind to the point of sexual entitlement, and I felt justified in crossing the line into physical infidelity. It destroyed my family, and I let it happen. It isn't porn's fault; it's mine because I can look back now with a clear head and see God-provided avenues for me to come completely clean. I came clean on most, but not all; we cannot partially surrender. I lacked the courage to fight entirely. It was the most crucial. When my ex-wife and I were in marriage counseling, I came clean about my porn but not my physical infidelity. This book is me coming completely clean in the hopes to save just one family from the rapacious grasp of porn.

In 2008, according to the book "Click: What Millions of People Do Online and Why It Matters" by Bill Tancer, 40,634 websites distributed pornography. Free porn websites comprise 70-80% of the online adult material typically used to bait users to paysites. Worldwide pornography revenue in 2006 was $97.06 billion. Of that, approximately $13 billion was in the United States (Internet Filter Review, 2006). Every second, $3,075.64 is spent on pornography, 28,258 Internet viewers view pornography, and 372 Internet users are typing adult search terms into search engines. Every 39 minutes, a new pornographic video is made in the United States.[ii]

According to the Journal of Adolescent Health, extended exposure to pornography leads to:

- An exaggerated preconception of sexual activity in
- society
- Diminished trust between intimate couples

- The abandonment of the hope of sexual monogamy
- A false belief that promiscuity is the natural state
- Confidence that abstinence and sexual inactivity are unhealthy
- Pessimism about love or the need for affection between partners
- An idea that marriage is sexually confining
- Lack of attraction to family and child-raising [iii]

Among middle-aged to young men, it would be hard to find someone who hasn't viewed online pornography but even harder to get them to talk openly and honestly in a church setting. One of the world's most popular porn sites, Porn Hub, reported the average millennial-aged male porn session lasts about nine minutes.

The average age of young people who have sex for the first time is seventeen years old. This means the average boy has had about 1,400 porn sessions before having real-life sex. When this critical period gets hijacked by watching copious amounts of online porn, men can suffer from what has been called "sexual anorexia" or difficulty having sex with a real partner; real naked women become substandard porn.

What effect this must-have on the women that have to compete with images and videos of strangers. Christians and leaders in the church are genuinely trying to do the right thing. As I have heard it said many times, in recovery, it takes an addict to help an addict; it takes a sinner to help a sinner.

Unfortunately, most Christians do not have a viable understanding of sin addiction or, most importantly, recovery. Just as that man told me not to buy the alcohol when I reached out to him, he did the best he could. He never wholly understood recovery as he never experienced this in his own life. We need to break the silence and shame of pornography. As followers of Christ, you have experienced the grip of porn's hold materialize the discipleship of Christ among fellow sufferers to come out and aid one another. I can fully relate to the pull of pornography and how it drags one down to sickness of self-pleasure and soothing outside of what God had planned for us. Porn makes us a slave, but even worse than that, it does it in silence. Not everyone is tempted with the same sins, and I have never found it exciting to gamble. As each of us has our spiritual gifts, we also have our spiritual handicaps. In recovery from those sins, we break the cycle and turn those liabilities into assets.

Culpability breaks the cycle of shame and loneliness. When someone shares their personal story with a trusted ally, it brings everything out into the light. Porn will not thrive out in the open. Our secrets flourish in the dark. I was at a men's retreat recently and shared my story openly and honestly. I was giving the standard Christian answer from Romans 3:23, *"For all have sinned and fall short of the glory of God" (NIV)*. I had just dumped my guts to men I only knew for several hours and was given a check-in block response. One man courageously shared he was part of his girlfriend from high school having two abortions. I have grown accustomed to sharing openly from my years in recovery rooms. The other men felt comfortable enough to let themselves become vulnerable enough to air out their secrets. I listened to their stories and found so many areas where our stories overlapped. Not all the deeds but the feelings of remorse and hopelessness.

It was his first time, and I am in awe of his bravery to do such. The next time won't be as hard, and that shame loses power with each time. Our liabilities become assets under the grace of Jesus; with courage, he can put us in the perfect situation to share his story to someone who needs it at the right time, and he may save an unborn baby with his personal testimony. When we become open and honest, we feel vulnerable, but we are mighty. God always picks the losers and outcasts from Moses to Paul; none were first picks by man's standards. Their inadequacies and flaws were exposed and used for his plan. Our secrets keep us in perpetual sickness, but the stones can now be used to throw in the devil's face when revealed.

On November 10, 2005, in the United States Senate Testimony of Jill N. Manning, m.s.hearing on pornography's impact on marriage & the family subcommittee on the constitution, civil rights and property rights committee on judiciary United States Senate Dr. Jill Manning was quoted as saying "The Internet is transforming the experience of growing up in America. It is also transforming the Job of being a parent in America. The Internet brings the world—the good, the bad, and the ugly—to the American family's doorstep. It brings the ruins of ancient Athens to that doorstep, but it also brings the red-light district of Bangkok." I am not that old but old enough to remember the encyclopedia set that adorned my living room; all the information needed was in there. Now the world is at our fingertips, the good and the bad. As quoted from the Spiderman comics, "with great power comes great responsibility."

I am not suggesting we scream the evils of porn and lust from the pulpit every Sunday; it is a very adult topic. Discretion and reason should always be the guide, but don't be naïve and foolhardy to think those innocent-looking kids you see all dolled up for church aren't already exposed to porn. My parents had no idea I was looking at porn magazines as early as I did, and that was before the Internet.

Dr. Jill Manning also testified in her research that pornography consumption is associated with the following six trends:

1. Increased marital distress

2. Decreased marital intimacy and sexual satisfaction
3. Infidelity
4. Increased appetite for more graphic types of pornography and sexual activity associated with abusive, illegal, and unsafe practices
5. Devaluation of monogamy, marriage, and child-rearing
6. An increasing number of people are struggling with compulsive and addictive sexual behavior.[iv]

      I have been a regular church attendee for over a decade and a half. I can only recall three sermons in front of the congregation where the pastor had touched on the subject. With these numbers and the impact that is almost undeniable, why the silence? I have talked to two preachers who were courageous enough to admit their struggles openly with pornography. When gay marriage was the hot topic of the land, I remember some very fiery southern Baptist sermons on how gay marriage would tear this country apart. All would applaud the courage of the preacher but the audience all agreed with him, I still fail to see the courage in talking about hard subjects in safe places. Yet while I was in the pew listening, I suspected I wasn't the only one who was secretly looking at porn every night after everyone when to bed. It might even have been that preacher.

      I was a church member for six years in one church, and I can remember three marriages were dissolved because of infidelity, one of them being my own. I can loosely recall 94 people attended church each week just from passing by the weekly attendance roster. Based on my rough math with,
say, four people per household, that's twelve people. $12/94=12.76\%$ of the people in the congregation are affected by divorce. To follow along with what Dr. Jill Manning[v] testified, 2/3 of divorces pornography played a significant role in my rough math $8/94 = 8.5\%$ of the congregation is seriously affected by pornography. The

silence from the pastors, if 8.5% of the assembly came down with diarrhea, absolute and definitive actions would have been taken. Suppose one were to realize if we change the words of COVID-19 with porn epidemic and as serious of a response would be given to fight sexual sin in lust. Envision a world in our churches that men could discuss freely and with the strictest confidence their struggle with sexual temptation amongst each other. Since D-day, I have become an active member of the Samson Society. The Samson Society is a fellowship of Christian men who are serious about recovery from sexual sin. It has proven to be a blessing because I now am not alone in my struggle and no longer feel isolated. Weakness in the church is acting fine even when you are not fine.

According to Nate Larkin, one of the Samson Society founders, in his book Beyond Accountability, *"Addiction we now know is invariably rooted in trauma. A person who is overwhelmed by feelings of inadequacy, terror, or loneliness will naturally reach for anything capable of calming those feelings."* [vi] In countless recovery meetings, I have heard that the consumption of a substance, whether drugs or alcohol is only the symptom. The real problem drives us to escape; I can easily understand my drinking, but I need to come to terms with my thirst for lust. Porn is no different from lust's desire in a country and time where we have everything beyond the wildest imaginations of those before us. Our
sexual envy drives us to lust, which reduces women to mere objects.

Pornography will educate us in ways that our parents and our faith have not; it will fill the holes of sexuality that we shy away from discussing. I could easily lull myself into a false sense of security into thinking once I have eradicated my porn use and infidelity that all is well without thoroughly and pray fully exploring the background and what was driving it. Porn and lust weren't the problem but had become the most powerful solution in my life. It solved a silent problem, like using a hand grenade to kill mice in your home; it kills the mice but destroys your home as well. One cannot even begin to search for the mice unless we admit to ourselves that there is a problem.

The loneliest orgasm one can feel is alone; that isn't how God intended it; it is to be shared. Staring at images of people you don't know doing things to each other you wish you were doing when your wife is sleeping is a sad state. I was in for far too long, and we cannot keep silent that far too many Christians find themselves in the same state, with nobody that they can turn to and be completely candid in private about their struggle. Far too many preachers are running their congregations by Facebook approval and keeping the peace. I am a Christian who is prone to vast sin and has a jaded past, and the church's formalities and pleasantries have kept me in religious fantasy land. That may work for many Christians, but not me. I need to be around fallible Christians, or else I shall repeat the past. Proverbs 28:13 tells us, *"Whoever conceals their sins does not prosper, but the one who confesses and renounces them finds mercy" (NIV)*.

In the kid's book "There's No Such Thing As A Dragon" by Jack Kent, Billy Bixbee was surprised when he woke up one morning and found a dragon in his room. It was a small dragon about the size of a kitten. The dragon wagged its tail happily when Billy patted its head. Billy went downstairs to tell his mother. "There's no such thing as a dragon!" said Billy's mother. And she said it as she meant it. Billy went back to his room and began to dress. The dragon came close to Billy and wagged its tail. But Billy didn't pat it. If there's no such thing as something, it's silly to pat it on the head. Billy washed his face and hands and went down to breakfast. The dragon went along. It was bigger now, almost the size of a dog. The dragon grew and grew each time Billy and his mother denied the dragon's existence. The dragon began growing quickly to the point of overtaking the entire house and wearing the house as though it were a turtle shell. It wasn't until his father returned home he finally acknowledged that there is a dragon. The dragon shrank and shrank until it was again the size of a kitten. Not all situations have to end terribly. Not everything turns into a dragon consuming our home. But every dragon that destroys a home started as a "little dragon" then sat on the table and looked you in the eye, begging to be noticed.[vii]

We cannot ignore the dragon being in denial and is very much a secret life. We hid from what is in front of us. Carl Jung says, *"That which we need the most will be found where we least want to look."*[viii] Do we deny the existence of a problem to avoid unpleasant effort? The realization that if this problem is not addressed today, at some point, you will be forced to address it. And you might not be in the best of shape to address it in the future.

Once pornography enters a marriage, its effects are often irreversible. A 2002 report by a consortium of attorneys reported that 68% of their divorce cases involved one party meeting a new lover through the Internet, and 56% involved one party obsessed with Internet pornography. But the death of a marriage is not instantaneous. It begins with the individual engaged in pornography, becoming less satisfied and happy with their marriage. Often a spouse seeks online pornography because

of loneliness, boredom, or even anger. The availability of comfortable stimulation is used to release stress. The spouse becomes addicted to the process of obtaining pornography, as with any addictive drug, pornography forms new neural networks in the brain.[ix]

Porn becomes the dragon in the room nobody wants to admit it's there.

Experimenting with pornography is never without repercussions. Once those images enter the man's mind, it has entered the marriage. It is impossible to look at pornography and not sin; those images once thrust into a man's mind forever change his relationship. The first casualty of this behavior and the longest to repair is trust. The marriage is forever altered as the images challenge the very covenant of marriage. The man's attention is taken away from the very one he was supposed to become one flesh through. Porn, most times, is the gateway to future sexual misconduct. It lays the groundwork for more and more because once the dependence on sexuality is placed outside of the marriage, it takes more and more to satisfy him.

Once porn entered my head, I can see the snowball formed, which created the avalanche that engulfed my family on D-day. Solomon, the wisest man ever, spoke extensively in Proverbs about sexual immorality that rings just as accurate today as in the Old Testament. Proverbs 6:26-27 states, *"For a prostitute will bring you to poverty but sleeping with another man's wife will cost you your life. Can a man scoop a flame into his lap and not have his clothes catch on fire?" (NLT)* When we play with the fire of porn and sexual immorality, we always get burned. It may not be today, but there are still consequences to deviation from God's image of sex. God's
vision of sex is fantastic and beautiful and wasn't intended to be what I have used it for. Sex isn't just physical, but I had reduced my sexuality to my genitals.

What is gambled with when porn is used to fill a void is not worth it. I live alone apart from my family because I didn't follow God's law and exercise basic decency and courage to let that demon control me. Lust doesn't make you hate God, but it enables you to forget

God. We begin to forget the things that mattered. Lust is deceptive, and the most resounding lie it tells you is that it isn't a lie. It fanned the flames of my rationalizations and excuses that I was justified in my actions. These same justifications were used when my lust brought me to a physical affair.

The church is on its heels with sexual immorality, and we are playing defense and choosing to ignore the problem. We are losing and losing badly. The devil is winning; internet pornography is one of his craftiest inventions. I am grateful I can talk openly about my struggles with pornography and my infidelity in many ways. I have nothing to lose and yet everything to gain. We cannot fight a dragon unless we first acknowledge its existence. I don't care to be the tie-clad smiling Christian anymore; trying to be a good Christian man nearly killed me. I almost took my own life several times because of shame and guilt. I just don't care anymore; I am the worst of sinners. I have let porn and my sexual sin destroy my family.

I am not the only one; there are many men like me, more than you could imagine. I have heard estimates as high as 80% percent of men struggle with porn in some way[26]. That's someone you know, a father, brother, uncle, pastor, deacon. The more I talk about my struggles, the more people open up to their battles. Let's quit playing the quiet
game of defense; I suggest we go on the attack. It's time for
some offense; let us talk honestly and in confidence. In the men's group's, women's group's, Bible

[26] "The Most Up-to-Date Pornography Statistics," Covenant Eyes (Covenant Eyes, January 25, 2021), https://www.covenanteyes.com/pornstats/.

study over the phone; porn's power is its silence. I know what I have done, and I am paying for it, and especially my family. I hope and pray they can all look at me with pride again. I am tired of wallowing in shame. My Lord and Savior, Jesus Christ, forgives me and loves me; if you still think less of me, I don't care. I have a mission and an aim to shine the light on the boogie man destroying lives.

In Jude 1:7, it says, *"In a similar way, Sodom and Gomorrah and the surrounding towns gave themselves up to sexual immorality and perversion. They serve as an example of those who suffer the punishment of eternal fire" (NIV).*

## 12 FIGHT

Immediately following D-day, many people would tell me, "if you truly love your family, fight for them." I did everything I could to change her mind to get her to reconsider reconciliation. They all failed miserably, and my reaction was to blame her for not wanting to save the marriage and not forgiving me. But upon honest reflection, I realize how wrong I indeed was. Reconciliation is a battle that is fought after the war is over; it can be helpful but is a long shot. I was not correct in any feeling of entitlement to any reconciliation. After what I did to my ex-wife and my family, I genuinely don't deserve any reconciliation and have frankly got way more than I feel I deserve from them, which is pure grace. If I dislike or approve of someone's reaction to my behavior, I shouldn't have acted like a selfish child.

I should have fought the fight I had while I was in the ring if I genuinely valued them. My actions post-D-day should have been done before I stepped out of my marriage. Once the bell is rung, the round is over, but that doesn't mean we can't fight. But, in many ways, it's already decided the battle is simply over. I became involved in a Christian men's group. I am seeing so many men on there, laying themselves at the mercy of everyone to keep what they have a good chance of losing, and often, they do anyway. There is a fine line between just groveling to keep what you feel entitled to and a truly repentant heart. Even if you are genuinely remorseful, you are not entitled to anything. Living your life with integrity is simple. If you're married, don't screw people you aren't married to; there will be severe consequences if you do. And the worst part, especially your children, will pay for that more than the cheater if you don't see that you are still acting like a selfish ass. I threw plenty of Hail Mary passes post-D-day, and the game was over.

If you find yourself where your spouse has forgiven, you better be prepared to eat a lot of crap because it is yours. Take it with a smile, and don't cry about how it's shoveled or the repetition or spoon amount. Suck it up, be a man, quit crying and complaining about what she is and isn't doing. She may not have had a halo, but they didn't do the horizontal mambo with someone else, which is a big deal; dignified deceit is a myth. Looking at images of other women having sex is doing nothing to help your marriage. It is hurting it; get real, find serious help. Being an addict is not an excuse. It's an explanation. I decided based on myself because I felt entitled and lacked the moral character to correct the problems, sort of stupid to cry about it after. I got caught and felt cheated out of my shot to keep my family when I didn't truly value it when I had it. Often, whining is just anger through a smaller hole, and the offense needs to rest in its appropriate place at the cheater's feet, which is me. When we have wronged others, playing the victim is like blaming the comb for our baldness, pretty silly any way you slice it.

My ex-wife was not a perfect wife, and we had many issues that went back to my days of drinking that we never resolved. We went to counseling, and things got better, and we were working through many issues. I believe we would have worked it all out because we were both fighting for our marriage; well, she was entirely. I held back and didn't come clean about my infidelity; why only cowardice. I used to believe that revealing something that will damage someone would be futile if not necessary. It even says in the Big Book of Alcoholics Anonymous, *"…but we cannot disclose anything to our wives or our parents which will hurt them and make them unhappy. We have no right to save our own skin at another person's expense. Such parts of our story we tell someone who will understand yet be unaffected. The rule is we must be hard on our self, but always considerate of others."* [27]

I am in no way knocking a movement that has saved millions upon millions of lives including mine; I am only stating that I no longer feel this way. If I had dared to reveal my infidelity while my ex-wife and I were in counseling, it would not have been pretty, and we might have still gotten divorced. The revelation of it would have been on my terms. We would have skipped the whole drug-induced, rage-filled psycho ex-lover coming to my front door. I wouldn't have wished that on my worst enemy. It would not have been pretty and nasty timing, but it would have been in counseling and on my terms. I was too much of a narcissist and wasn't entirely in on fixing my marriage, as she was. If I indeed were, I would have told her, and not a day has gone by that I wish I had since I have realized that. She wasn't a perfect wife, but she was mine, and I didn't truly treasure her, so I lost her and my family. God is not always on our side; I believe he was on hers post-D-day, leading her away because he knew I didn't deserve her. Proverbs 6:32-33 states, *"But a man who commits adultery has no sense; whoever does so destroys himself. Blows and disgrace are his lot, and his shame will never be wiped away" (NIV).*

There is indeed evil in this world, and certain people seem to do nothing but destroy. Proverbs 7 tells the tale of an adulterous woman; if you are currently having an affair on your spouse, I want to honestly ask you what type of person with full knowledge you are married engages and pursues a married man. My experience is not one of high emotional stability and must be avoided at all costs. You might even be lying that you are married and

[27] Bill W., Aaron Cohen, and Bill W., Alcoholics Anonymous: the Original Big Book, 12 Steps, Guides, and Prayers, the Story of How Many Thousands of Men and Women Have Recovered from Alcoholism (Twelve Step Study Guides Publishing, 2015).

loving the excitement of pretending to be single. If you think you will

not get caught, many men smarter than you tried the same thing and failed. Is your family worth the gamble?

Ecclesiastes 1:9 tells us, *"What has been will be again, what has been done will be done again; there is nothing new under the sun" (NIV)*. Adultery back then was the same as it is now; it only destroys, it never creates. Solomon, the wisest man ever, couldn't control his desire for women, which led him to break God's law and marry multiple women and take foreign women as his wives. Then his wives seduced him to worship false gods. Solomon's desire led him to commit adultery as well, and then idolatry. Solomon never repented. His father, King David, repented and changed how he fought to be a man of God and published his wrong in psalms for all to see.

Solomon had all the wisdom in the world but being smart doesn't mean a hill of beans if we cannot apply it in our lives; it means nothing. Knowledge isn't power; knowledge applied is. I had spent a considerable amount of time in recovery, which arguably is self-help groups. I had heard and reheard many buckets of wisdom that I could pull from my thought bank at any given time. I would half-joke in recovery rooms that many people in the church would believe me to be incredibly wise. Still, I was just regurgitating common sayings that most people would say in recovery meetings. I was quoting things I had heard or read in recovery literature in many areas of my life in many instances. My point being I began to believe I was smart. As Socrates famously said, *"I am the wisest man alive, for I know one thing, and that is that I know nothing."*

Knowledge without humility is just hot air with an ego. As I have heard it said in recovery for years, E.G.O. stands for "easing God out." I had overcome alcoholism and porn addiction and ended an affair, but it means nothing without honesty. I had forgotten two divine realities: that he is loving and also judging. The timing of his judgment is in his capable hands. I had forgotten that nobody among humanity would get away with the evil that he does. The wages of sin—death—is a reality (Romans 6:23). I cannot allow myself to forget that God is judging. It is a continuous process, and we are not aware of the present, unseen penalties that the evil person may already be paying.

I have learned from my story that you never get away with anything, period—the evil we do to others even in secret we pay for. In honest reflection, I can see God had given me plenty of opportunities to fix my marriage, and I took advantage of many of them. I read, prayed, upped my spiritual game, prayed more, was more open and honest with my wife. I ended my infidelities, and we began working on each other, and last year was the best. Suppose this sounds like rationalizing and covering up sin because it is. You don't get half points for effort; Jesus even said in Mark 10:8, "'and the two will become one flesh.' So they are no longer two, but one flesh" (NIV). If something is in your flesh and it is harmful to you and can kill you, that's cancer, and cutting out cancer to save the rest can never be done in secret.

Your wife may be a terrible human being and may very well treat you awful but screwing someone else and hiding it is far worse. And looking at naked pictures of other people certainly doesn't help; get honest and fix yourself before throwing stones or even boulders on her. In 2021, there are many resources available in the land of plenty of this great country if one will go to any lengths to fix their marriage. Even a quick google search will net thousands of books, and any counseling one could need. Doing something for your marriage is always better than nothing. After D-day, I got sincere quickly because the woman I once scorned for not treating me a certain way in the marriage as I "stayed late after the recovery meeting," I would have done anything to keep her, and my pain caused that honesty. The irony is if I were honest like that in my marriage, we would most likely still be married. Anytime in my life, I have strayed from Christ, I have paid the price. If your wife is malicious, look at the mirror; what kind of ass are you to shape her behavior? Be honest; you can't lie to Jesus or the man in the mirror, that man in the mirror looking back at you is your most immense accountability. Take a few minutes and look at yourself in the mirror and be completely honest; if you try, you might be surprised what you unravel.

There are practically counselors on every street corner in most towns itching to take your money. They accept most insurance, and even if you have to pay out of pocket, it's still cheaper than alimony and child support. What price are you willing to pay for a healthy marriage? You thought at one point that person you shackled yourself to was important. You can't put a price on some things, and marriage is one of them. If you want to stay married, then put your money where your mouth is. What price are you willing to pay, and what length are you ready to go to be the man your family deserves? Since D-day, I am amazed by how blind I was to what I should have done with so much time in honest reflection. I was fighting, but my aim was off. Quit believing for one second what you see in others is accurate. We do not know what others are struggling with unless we earnestly and honestly try to understand from their perspective. To do that, I must do something that I am trying to get better with. I genuinely need to put that other person's needs and desires above my own. That usually begins with closed lips; I can honestly see how much time I spent telling my ex-wife what she should do to fix our marriage instead of actively listening. It's easy to listen to the things we want to hear but tough to listen to things we disagree with. I would immediately become defensive and try to defend my bolstering ego and win her over to see how I saw the problem. The inevitable result was her hesitance to share anything with me genuinely. Everyone has a voice, even if it conflicts with our ego.

I used to sponsor a man who was chairman of the deacons at his church and director over all the Sunday school classes. Only being a Christian for a few years, I was very immature in my faith, but I was engulfed in recovery language. Outside the rooms of recovery, I would struggle with communicating my faith. He was more than willing to point this out at any chance he could to disparage my faith and to esteem his. I was years away from crossing the line into physical infidelity and failed to heed the warning of his story. He was an infrequent drug and alcohol user; he would sometimes go on a binge yet go weeks without a drop, maintaining his social standing. When he went back out, it would go on for days. He was an avid porn user, but what was particularly odd when he did "go back out," he would get a couple of beers, and once loosened up, he would get the itch to buy some crack. Once he made it to that point, he was off to the closest strip club to pick up all the strippers he could by enticing them with drugs. They would hole up in a sleazy motel until he melted his checking account and savings like spring snow.

Broke and battered, he would crawl back home and somehow got his wife to accept him back again until he went back on the bandwagon again. He would call me, and I would help him get back into recovery again. From the outside, he seemed like a strong man of faith. I once caught him stroking an old ladies' hand in Walmart. This lady was a member of his church, and he was praying with her about something mere hours after he had confessed to me about being holed up with several hookers for the weekend. I am not judging him for praying for that woman; he did the right thing, but I know he got suckered into believing his crap he shoveled to everyone, just as I did years later. I have fought my whole life in one direction or another. His wife eventually wised up and started making demands that he shaped up or shipped out, and he chose the path of least resistance and left. I bump into her at least a couple of times a year. She always speaks to me, and we exchange pleasantries but never discuss her ex-husband. As I have come to know, shame covers not only ourselves but its darkest over those we love. His addiction and lust destroyed his marriage, and I failed to heed his warning. I solely focused on his substance addiction, ignoring what was piggybacking his drug and alcohol addiction, which was lust.

I spent years fighting alcohol. Alcohol distorted my mind so much I had to fight to stay sober. It was challenging to get sober in the original recovery program, but the people in recovery saved my life. Getting honest about and tackling my porn use was difficult; it was a daily battle fighting the temptation. I changed up my recovery meeting, started associating with people who struggled like me, and did many things to clean up my behavior. I was becoming more honest about my struggles with people in the church. I took severe measures to change my whole daily routine to ease healthy spiritual and physical wellbeing. When I ended my physical affair, I thought my problems were behind me. I have and was actively fighting my demons. Believing God would bless my efforts was foolhardy; all exertions are only half measure without complete honesty.

I was fighting but, in many ways, was aiming at the wrong target. As the old Baptist hymnal states, "I surrender all," I only surrendered some and wasn't willing to sacrifice everything to the will of the Father. I never looked her dead in her eyes and told her I was ready to fight to my death to keep her. I admitted my affair, but only after a scorned high woman had told her in her kitchen. As I have heard it said in recovery for years, we can learn humility and honesty, or it can be taught to us. I never suspected how valid those words are. I was fighting for my marriage, but I held one key element out. We cannot fight unless we have the courage, and I lacked the character; to fight all the way and come clean about everything to her. I may still have been divorced, but my fight would have been a good one, and I believe in my heart, God would have blessed my real fight.

The point of this chapter is to shed light on my inept and ego-driven fight in my marriage. And my realization of the futility of my battle plan. God isn't always on our side, and despite the best of our intentions, but without authentic motives that involve prayer and Jesus, we may be doomed to failure. A humbling pill I have had to swallow is Jesus may have been answering my ex-wife's blessings and not mine. He may very well have seen the result of my efforts, and I lost them because I was not worthy of them. He had given me so many chances to come clean about everything, and I always did just enough to get by. I became honest in pain and humiliation, and that's what it took regrettably, but that isn't Jesus" fault. That blame rests totally on my shoulders. When a man knows the right thing to do but doesn't do it, he is sinning.

Luke 8:17 tells us, *"For there is nothing hidden that will not be disclosed and nothing concealed that will not be known or brought out into the open" (NIV)*. We never get away with anything, period; what we bury today will rear its ugly head tomorrow. With social media, we are lulled into a false sense of security, thinking we can hide from those we care for our secret desires. We are as sick as our secrets; I learned this in recovery. I knew this, but I thought what I concealed would never come to light. It came to light in the most unpleasant ways; we believe we buried our deceit bodies deep enough and in perfect spots. I think we're only fooling ourselves. It is self-centered and prideful to think we are unique or cunning enough to overcome what man has done since the beginning of time.

I was talking to a recently divorced woman, I suspect, because of my openness in revealing my own story. I felt open enough to disclose that she had noticed since her divorce, several married men reached out to her on Facebook and especially on Snapchat. This woman's marriage ended because of her husband's infidelity. She had men either posing as single or flat out propositioning an affair. These men are not savory characters but men who appear to be great pillars in the community that lead a double life. Her high school sweetheart kept making attempts through Snapchat. His double life, aided by technology, will be found out. As it says in Luke 12:2-3, *"There is nothing concealed that will not be disclosed or hidden that will not be made known. What you have said in the dark will be heard in the daylight, and what you have whispered in the ear in the inner rooms will be proclaimed from the roofs" (NIV).*

If we are unhappy in our marriage, what are we going to do about it? I admit the thrill of the chase and lure of the fantasy is a powerful intoxicant and one that had bitten me. After years of working, raising kids, and building a family, marriage becomes a burden. The thought and allure of an escape are too much for many men, including me. The passion may be gone, but what did I do to foster love, and how much of the expectations I put on my spouse are false? I never took my wife to one marriage conference. I planned a one-weekend getaway vacation to Boone, North Carolina; she turned it into a family vacation, and I cried about that for years. Why didn't I schedule another one? Because it was easier to play the victim and use excuses to run around on my wife. I felt fully justified while I was having an affair; drunk with a head full of rationalization, we can sign off on almost anything.

I was fighting but in the wrong direction. Conflict can be beneficial in a marriage; if she didn't want to read books, go to marriage conferences, or go back to marriage counseling. I should have fought with her until I wore her down enough that she would go. If he spent the time-fighting in his marriage that he spends hunting the women who will make him whole and satisfied, the women he is running from would most likely become the women he is chasing.

At one point, we thought that person we married was the best thing, and we made a conscious decision to be with that person. They excited us at one point, and they can excite us again if we can only try. Having your wife of twenty years tell you she has a date, and she likes him, and he is a good man just plain sucks. It's a gut punch that hurts, and the silence from my daughter has been deafening. When to the point of frustration, the crowding of responsibilities, trying to fulfill your role as a husband, is replaced with the thunderous silence of not being needed anymore. They all are forging their new life minus you. I have nobody to blame but myself. I was weak when I should have been strong. I didn't fight for marriage when it counted, and I lost them because of my lack of character and selfishness.

When the family splits, no matter the cooperation and civility, the family unit is fractured instead of a team effort to keep the family moving. The tasks that are historically done in tandem now befall upon one. It usually falls upon the innocent party forced to bear the burden. Helping with homework, arranging rides to all activities, disciplining, cleaning up, and infinities of small tasks are compounded for years to come. The lashes of infidelity are one of a thousand little, tiny insults. Marriage is like a well-oiled machine. If one gear is taken away, the engine can never run with the same efficiency and puts a strain on the strongest of women. After the initial explosion and the dust settles, and the new normal is put into effect, the pressure on one parent left from the other's sin is an insult that hits daily for years to come. If you are married, I can only plea with you to do the following.

Go down swinging with everything you have. Don't throw in the towel on your marriage. Look yourself in the mirror and pray with gut-level honesty to find your weakness. Fight against your faults; fight to tell her everything. Stand and fight against the temptation to make peace and stuff your feelings. You can't control anyone in this world but yourself, be in control; don't succumb to your emotions. If you do make amends quickly and honestly, be open and honest always. You can only do one thing, and that is the next right thing. Fight against feelings of inferiority, fear, and marital decay. She mattered to you once more than anything, so fight for the bride of your youth. Fight for your family; you count but only at your best. Go down swinging, give everything you got. When you are scared to tell her something you have been hiding from her, large or small, stand up and go forward tell her. Don't just tell her, reveal all your fears, and be who you are in front of her. Tell her what lengths you are willing to go to have victory; hold nothing back. Two things cannot occupy the same space simultaneously, fear and faith. Believe that the good Lord will bless you as you go into battle for your family, your tribe, and your bride. If you fight with all you have, you won't go down often. This fight isn't one round, and you fight this fight until the fight is done. Stay honest, stay humble, make the right choices, be loving, be teachable, and believe the Lord Jesus will be with you in this fight.

Go out in a blaze of glory, fighting with

everything: every ounce of energy, read books, listen instead of talking, don't defend yourself but actively listen. Schedule counseling, find a worthwhile pastor, go to treatment even if you don't want to. Buy the flowers, write the notes of encouragement. Spend the time making yourself mentally, physically, and spiritually more vital, not just for you but for them. Shut your mouth. Give every ounce of blood, sweat, and tears until your last breath. Then and only then can you put your sword back in its sheath and get on your knees in thanks and grace. Even if you lose, you fought with everything.

# 13 PRODIGAL

The natural beauty of all the Bible stories is their endurance of time and the fact they are short. The unnecessary is omitted, so they are cram-packed with deep meaning, and the parable of the prodigal son is no different; its power lingers with us. In the Parable of the Prodigal Son (Luke 15:11-31), there are three key players in the story, and each person can relate to one or more of the characters of the story. The older son, the father, and the younger son or prodigal son. I have, at one point or another in my life, being each one of the characters. Still, I have related to the prodigal son due to my straying from God either from alcoholism, pornography, and eventually physical infidelity. If we are all truly honest with ourselves, we have all been the three characters at one point in our life. The prodigal son, the classic story of the lost sheep who found his way with the faithful servant, the older brother who stayed home and did the right thing, and finally, the loving father who loves without reason resonates with me.

Luke 15:12-13 states, *"The younger one said to his father, 'Father, give me my share of the estate.' So he divided his property between them. "Not long after that, the younger son got together all he had, set off for a distant country and there squandered his wealth in wild living" (NIV).* The son's share of his father's estate was prematurely given to the youngest son upon his request. This is no small feat to give to one, especially if it took a lifetime to accumulate. Sacrifice is the representation of the idea that foregoing pleasure now is a successful strategy. When engaging in sacrifice, our forefathers began to act out that something of better value might be attained in the future by giving up something of value in the present. Your demise might be staved off through work or the sacrifice of the now to benefit later. It represents so much more than that. The youngest son did precisely the opposite of what the father had done when he indulged in the present at tomorrow's expense.

I suspect that the son knew what his father had freely given up, but his selfish desires overruled this knowledge for the short term. His propensity to squabble those years of sacrifice for fleeting interim desires freely was telling of his immaturity. His shortsightedness unfolds as the story progresses; we can only suspect it wasn't a feeble amount with the amount of repentance the son had felt after his misuse of it. In our brokenness, we begin to see with clarity; the son knew he deserved to be amongst the filth and slop of pigs, He was given his share of his father's estate, and he squandered it on immoral living. Every ounce of his claim was something he didn't earn; his father did; it was years of sacrifice, which his father freely gave to him. When we make even a penny, it is a symbol of us trading something for that penny. We earned it somehow, so we forego what we want today and invest the labor to gain something of value. I think we cheapen the lesson and not take the story seriously enough if we don't value the father's sacrifice in the story. The amount isn't necessary, but we can assume it was at least multiple years of honest hard labor to accumulate. The father sacrificed his current desire to invest it in tomorrow by holding on to it and yet lovingly, almost without regard, gave his son's share.

Luke 15: 14 states, *"After he had spent everything, there was a severe famine in that whole country, and he began to be in need. So he went and hired himself out to a citizen of that country, who sent him to his fields to feed pigs" (NIV).* When we buy anything, especially something we desire, we feel better, and we feel good. We are a big shot for a moment; we know that buyer's high is fleeting. I have never seen anyone frown after buying a new car. Stuff makes us feel good, and we know it's temporary, but at what expense do we do this? In the great feasts in our lives, there is usually a famine in our lives after the glitter and glaze die down. There was always the initial excitement, the adventure in my addictions, whether porn, alcohol, and even my affair. But after sparkle dies down, the famine always comes. The excitement faded after they already had their hooks in me, and the deprivation began. I believe we all go through famines in our lives, periods after great feasts where the land is barren and void of hope.

Luke 15:16-17 states, *"He longed to fill his stomach with the pods that the pigs were eating, but no one gave him anything. "When he came to his senses, he said, 'How many of my father's hired servants have food to spare, and here I am starving to death!"* (NIV). What we once in merry times turned our noses at in our feasts become diamonds in our famines. After the son decides to go to his father, humbled and humiliated, broken by his sin, and willing to do anything and go to any lengths to accept anything his father could provide, he was thirsty for relief. He had been beaten by his actions and was paying for them. He was sincere in his repentance and was willing to, as it is said in Verse 16, eat what the pigs had eaten. He was longing for it and then came to his senses and realized how good he had it, and when one realizes the comfort we once possessed, we cannot help but look at the disparity we currently find ourselves. It is easy to imagine light when surrounded by darkness.

Luke 15:18-19 states, *"I will set out and go back to my father and say to him: Father, I have sinned against heaven and against you. I am no longer worthy to be called your son; make me like one of your hired servants"* (NIV). The younger son's guilt and penance had driven him to the point of despair to go home with his pride beaten back. The reckless son went out to discover himself because he thought he would find meaning in pleasure, which he learned was a helpless pursuit. In one sense, the prodigal son understands more than his brother since to understand the light; one must understand the dark. Whether we admit it to ourselves or not, the darkness that rests in all of us, the tug of sin, tugs at us all. He has stared into the pitiful darkness that is the pursuit of pleasure at the expense of virtue. We sometimes must sell ourselves before we know our value.

The most beautiful part of the entire story for me is in Luke 15:20 states, *"So he got up and went to his father. "But while he was still a long way off, his father saw him and was filled with compassion for him; he ran to his son, threw his arms around him, and kissed him" (NIV).* After the youngest son's rebellion, the father's reaction is lovely; he not only went to him and loved him but "ran" to him. The father didn't wait for the son to approach him, but the father ran to his lost son. He ran and embraced him and kissed him, which is more potent than any words can precisely express.

Caught up in my self-created misery after D-day, my sin had separated me from everyone I loved, including God. I felt dejected and alone as I had never before in my life. I was at a crossroads, and in my desperation and desolation, I called out again as I had done on December 20, 2005. Jesus, help me, just help me. I can't go on. I immediately felt his presence; the pain didn't go away, but I knew he was there. I felt his love when I needed it most; I still had to pay the consequences of my sin as even I am today. The story never says that the younger son ever gets another share of the estate, but I believe he didn't get another share. The older brother probably retained his share, we always pay for our sin, but love and grace are free. If he was genuinely apologetic, being back in the light is enough to build for a better tomorrow.

After my stumbling back to Jesus, I felt his love, and a few men from my church reached out to me. Jesus was just like the father in the story; he ran when I came staggering back with my tail tucked between my legs like a misbehaved puppy. I can only think of the love that the father had for his youngest son. It wasn't a preacher who reached out to me; I didn't hear a word from him. It was men with who I had formed relationships within the church; it wasn't all the men I had developed relationships with, but it was enough; people are people and just as flawed as me, even if they don't admit it. I am eternally grateful to these men; they saved me. I must remember to form Christian relationships. We are only as strong as those we surround ourselves with. We cannot complain about any organization if we don't put in the relational effort.

Luke 15:21 states, *"The son said to him, 'Father, I have sinned against heaven and against you. I am no longer worthy to be called your son" (NIV).* The son recognized he not only betrayed his father but God himself; that is a profound difference. I have wronged so many people in my life; I have lied about things that mattered and things that didn't. I lied to get what I wanted and to make myself appear great when I wasn't. I have gotten caught in lies, and I have gotten away with lies. I have apologized to people and made amends to them for wronging them. Any absolute amends must include humility and profound, meaningful admission that our behavior is not only against man but God's law and His will for us. If we don't fully atone, we just worldly repent and don't get the fattened calf. We settled for the world's reward for atonement, which pales in comparison to God's.

Luke 15:22-24 states, *"But the father said to his servants, 'Quick! Bring the best robe and put it on him. Put a ring on his finger and sandals on his feet. Bring the fattened calf and kill it. Let's have a feast and celebrate. For this Son of mine was dead and is alive again; he was lost and is found.' So they began to celebrate" (NIV).* Upon hearing his son's heartfelt repentance, his father demanded immediately the best be brought to his son. Have any of us ever received something we didn't deserve? In my early recovery from alcoholism, I used to run or ride bikes to a noon meeting every Saturday; it was only a few miles and was always an excellent way to clear my head and enjoy the fresh air before a meeting. On this particular day, while walking through downtown Gaffney, I saw a guy sleeping on a bench.

He reeked of alcohol, and I saw his last night's drunk all over him, which most likely ended only a few hours before. As I passed the bench, he was waking up; it was apparent he passed out on the bench. He was in his mid-forties; he didn't appear to be homeless, and even now, I could pick him out of a crowd. Our eyes locked, and immediately I felt a connection because, at that moment, I knew how he felt down to the taste of the film that was in his mouth. I had passed out drunk in more than my share of public places only to be awakened and looked upon with disdain. But I was sure he didn't know he felt what it was like to be sober, feel free from addiction, and wake without the immediate craving to drink. I had woken up in so many places I didn't intend to succumb to my alcoholic-soaked brain. In that brief instant, I was taken immediately back to myself in my active alcoholism, which wasn't that long ago, and my response was an overcoming feeling of gratitude. I knew and still know I don't deserve to be free from my alcoholism, especially when I saw so many alcoholics/addicts not make it. December 20, 2005, I surrendered completely to Jesus, and he started me on a path of recovery, which was difficult. That morning on the run, I was reminded that Jesus, like the father, brought the loveliest things to me way beyond what I deserved. The fattened calf was brought at my feet, and I know I deserve pig slop in my heart.

Luke 15:25-27 states, *"Meanwhile, the older son was in*

*the field. When he came near the house, he heard music and dancing. So he called one of the servants and asked him what was going on. 'Your brother has come,' he replied, 'and your father has killed the fattened calf because he has him back safe and sound'" (NIV).* The older son was busy doing what was expected of him, and after a long day of labor, he was returning home and learned his wayward nitwit brother is getting a party of the likes he has never seen. If I am diligent in doing what I believe to be correct in my own life, I quickly jump onto my self-righteous high horse and cast stones on those who aren't toeing the line. The older brother judged his brother, and we can reasonably assume because his brother's sin was unacceptable to him. How often we all do the same thing.

A woman from one of the churches I attended was the victim of a brain aneurysm and nearly died. Her family was deeply involved in the church, and the church rallied around her family to show support. Anonymous financial donations were given to offset the financial strain on the family. Prayers, time, and money were thrown to help the family. The church came together to help that ailing family. The mother's recovery was miraculous. For weeks afterward, testimony upon testimony was given, testifying the power of prayer and Christian love. I am not chastising or criticizing; I merely want to propose that a body of believers such as my old church can rally around an entire family when something is as tragic as a brain aneurysm. Would it be possible for that same body to rally around a family where they have been touched by sin? If we replaced brain aneurysm for adultery or addiction in any form. I believe the answer lies in the reason the older son never embraced his younger brother. In prejudice, we are moved to love only in cases where the behavior is acceptable to us. That is the difference between the father and the older son. The father extended his love to his son in his sincere repentance, despite the offense. The older son was unwilling to accept his younger brother because it was outside his acceptable conduct boundaries.

Luke 15:28-30 states, *"The older brother became angry and refused to go in. So, his father went out and pleaded with him. But he answered his father, 'Look! All these years, I've been slaving for you and never disobeyed your orders. Yet you never gave me even a young goat so I could celebrate with my friends. But when this son of yours who has squandered your property with prostitutes comes home, you kill the fattened calf for him!' (NIV).* The younger brother made big mistakes but then committed fully to the wisdom of his father. The older brother shows his judgment by not being happy for his brother but instead wishing that a feast had been thrown for him. He questioned his father's love, and I feel we all can feel a little sad for the older brother's perception he was cheated, even refusing to go in. Jesus was a master storyteller because we never know what the older brother does; it's open-ended. We don't know if he comes and embraces his father and younger brother. When I am disturbed, it is because I find some fact of my life unacceptable to me. Serenity will escape me until I accept that person, place, thing, or situation as being exactly the way it is supposed to be at this moment.

We are all children of God, and we only see the part of the visible person. In their personal stories, everyone describes in their language, and from their point of view, they established their relationship with God. I was working one night on my part-time job, and a couple of crossdressers came into the store, and the snickers and sneers came out, and we all had a good laugh, and regrettably, so did I. I rang up what they had bought and began to feel guilty. Who am I to judge them? Some people wear their crazy on the outside, but most wear it inside deep to avoid ridicule. It's there in all of us whether we want to admit it or not; it's there all the same. It's easy and cowardly to judge others without looking at ourselves first.

The older brother did everything he was expected to do and yet missed the mark in the judgment of his brother; how many times have I been him, the prideful resolute one who can look down on others. With pride and arrogance always come with my judgment, it's effortless for me to pick apart others' Christianity and their walk. Still, if I am sincere, it is slightly intoxicating to play the victim and pass judgment on those who have wronged me. The afflictions that have been pushed upon us, real or imagined, are but a distraction from what we should be doing. C.S. Lewis once said God doesn't want something from us; he simply wants us.[x] That is the mark I miss because my aim is off; our obedience acts don't define our relationship. God judges my heart and my motives; beliefs are not worth much unless they are lived out in actions. Once we fall, we must always get back up; steel is more robust after it is heated and beaten; when we fall and get back up, we are stronger than those who have never fallen.

In the story of the Samaritan woman at the well, in John 4, there is a prolific story. The interaction between an outcast among outcasts and Jesus rings so true to me. Jesus revealed to her that he was the messiah and all she had done; she was lifted of her burden of guilt by Jesus and left her water pot. She was so excited to tell others of the good news of the messiah. In John 4 28-30, he says, *"Then, leaving her water jar, the woman went back to the town and said to the people, "Come, see a man who told me everything I ever did. Could this be the Messiah?" They came out of the town and made their way toward him" (NIV)*. Once our sin is revealed, it is cause for a celebration; we no longer have to evade the facts of our sin. We can then bask in the glow of forgiveness, and there is no shame there.

The prodigal son and the woman at the well know this, as I do.; There is absolute freedom with the skeletons of our closet swept out, for the world to see and be humble... People will try to throw that blanket of shame over us; you might be surprised by their secrets. There is nothing more substantial than a broken man who has rebuilt himself with God's help. Instead of wasting our lives worrying about what others are thinking, we must focus on being the best person we can be right now. What others think is irrelevant; only Christ matters. I must never forget tomorrow; every action has a tomorrow. How will I feel about what I am doing right now, tomorrow?

# BIBLIOGRAPHY

Allen, James. As a Man Thinketh. New York: St. Martin's Essentials, 2021.

Azad, Hasan. "'That Which We Need the Most Will Be Found Where We Least Want to Look." ~ Carl Jung." Medium. Medium, September 1, 2020. https://medium.com/@hasanazad/that-which-we-need-the-most-will-be-found-where-we-least-want-to-look-carl-jung-db6311c02f15#:~:text=%E2%80%9CThat%20which%20we%20need%20the,Jung%20%7C%20by%20Hasan%20Azad%20%7C%20Medium.

Coughlin, Paul. "No More Christian Nice Girl Quotes by Paul Coughlin." Goodreads. Goodreads. Accessed February 16, 2021.

Covey, Stephen R. The 7 Habits of Highly Effective People. London: Simon & Schuster UK Ltd., 2020.

DOSTOEVSKY, FYODOR. BROTHERS KARAMAZOV. S.l.: PICADOR, 2021.

Gibbons, Luke. "Serial Killer Ted Bundy Describes the Dangers of Pornography." CBN News, October 31, 2018. https://www1.cbn.com/cbnnews/us/2018/october/serial-killer-ted-bundy-describes-the-dangers-of-pornography.
Hedges, Chris. Empire of Illusion: The End of Literacy and the Triumph of Spectacle. New York, USA: Basic Books, 2010.

Larkin, Nate. "New Free EBook: Beyond Accountability

by Nate Larkin." Discipleship.org, September 14, 2017. https://discipleship.org/bobbys-blog/new-free-ebook-beyond-accountability-by-nate-larkin/.

Larkin, Nate. Samson and the Pirate Monks: Calling Men to Authentic Brotherhood. Nashville, TN: W Pub. Group, 2007.

Lewis, C. S. Mere Christianity. Harpercollins Publishers, 2017.

Manning, Brennan, John Blase, and Jonathan Foreman. Abba's Child: the Cry of the Heart for Intimate Belonging. Colorado Springs, CO: NavPress, 2015.

Manning, Brennan. The Ragamuffin Gospel. Colorado Springs, CO: Multnomah Books, 2015.

Manning, Brennan. The Wisdom of Tenderness: What Happens When God's Fierce Mercy Transforms Our Lives. Amazon. HarperSanFrancisco, 2004. \

Merton, Thomas. The Seven Storey Mountain. San Diego: Harcourt Brace, 1999.

Merton, Thomas. The way of Chuang Tzu. New York: Random House, 1992.
"The Most Up-to-Date Pornography Statistics." Covenant Eyes. Covenant Eyes, January 25, 2021. https://www.covenanteyes.com/pornstats/.

Nogales, Ana, and Laura Golden Bellotti. Parents Who Cheat: How Children and Adults Are Affected When Their Parents Are Unfaithful. Deerfield Beach, FL: Health Communications, 2009.

Manning, Jill C. Manning. Testimony of Jill C. Manning, m.s. Hearing on pornography's impact on marriage & the family subcommittee on the constitution, civil rights and property rights, committee on judiciary United States Senate. November 10, 2005, January 25, 2021, https://s3.amazonaws.com/thf_media/2010/pdf/ManningTST.pdf

Patrick, Charles. Pornography: Marriage's Silent Killer. Harmony Hill, 2014.

Schorn, Tracy. Leave a Cheater, Gain a Life: The Chump Lady's Survival Guide. Perseus Books Group, 2016.
Kent, Jack, There's No Such Thing as a Dragon (Golden book,2005)

Tancer, Bill. Click: What Millions of People Are Doing Online and Why It Matters. New York, NY: Hyperion, 2008.

W., Bill, Aaron Cohen, and Bill W. Alcoholics Anonymous: the Original Big Book, 12 Steps, Guides, and Prayers, the Story of How Many Thousands of Men and Women Have Recovered from Alcoholism. Twelve Step Study Guides Publishing, 2015.

Wilson, Gary. Your Brain on Porn: Internet Pornography and the Emerging Science of Addiction. Margate, Kent, United Kingdom: Commonwealth Publishing, 2017.
Zillmann, Dolf. "Influence of Unrestrained Access to Erotica on Adolescents' and Young Adults' Dispositions toward Sexuality." Journal of Adolescent Health 27, no. 2(2000): 41–44. https://doi.org/10.1016/s1054-139x(00)00137-3.

[i] "The Most Up-to-Date Pornography Statistics," Covenant Eyes (Covenant Eyes, January 25, 2021), https://www.covenanteyes.com/pornstats/.
[ii] Bill Tancer, Click:
[iii] Dolf Zillmann, "Influence of Unrestrained Access to Erotica on Adolescents' and Young Adults' Dispositions toward Sexuality," Journal of Adolescent Health
[iv] Manning, Jill C. Manning. Testimony of Jill C. Manning, m.s. Hearing on pornography's impact on marriage & the family subcommittee on the constitution, civil rights and property rights, committee on judiciary United States Senate. November 10, 2005, January 25, 2021, https://s3.amazonaws.com/thf_media/2010/pdf/ManningTST.pdf
[v] Manning, Jill C. Manning. Testimony of Jill C. Manning, m.s. Hearing on pornography's impact on marriage & the family subcommittee on the constitution, civil rights and property rights, committee on judiciary United States Senate. November 10, 2005, January 25, 2021,

https://s3.amazonaws.com/thf_media/2010/pdf/ManningTST.pdf

[vi] Nate Larkin, "New Free EBook: Beyond Accountability by Nate Larkin," Discipleship.org, September 14, 2017, https://discipleship.org/bobbys-blog/new-free-ebook-beyond-accountability-by-nate-larkin/.
[vii] Kent, Jack, "Theres no such thing as a dragon"(Golden book,2005)
[viii] Hasan Azad, "'That Which We Need the Most Will Be Found Where We Least Want to Look." ~ Carl Jung," Medium (Medium, September 1, 2020).
[ix] Charles Patrick, "Pornography: Marriage's Silent Killer" (Harmony Hill, 2014).

[x] C. S. Lewis, Mere Christianity (Harpercollins Publishers, 2017).
Zimbardo, Philip, and Gary Wilson. "How Porn Is Messing with Your Manhood." Skeptic.com, April 12, 2016.
https://web.archive.org/web/20160612212631/http://www.skeptic.com/reading_room/how-porn-is-messing-with-your-manhood/.

Thank you for reading My Book
Rick Levesque

Made in the USA
Columbia, SC
06 December 2021